# Our Ninian Park

## NINIAN PARK IN ITS FINAL YEAR

**MARK WATKINS**

First published 2012 by Wyndcliff

1 Eastern Business Park, St Mellons, Cardiff CF3 5EA

Design by Wyndcliff
www.wyndcliff.co.uk

Printed by HSW Print
www.hswprint.co.uk

ISBN 978 0 9572055 0 5

*This book is dedicated to my father, Tony, who first took me to Ninian Park in 1973 and to my mother, Dorothy, who has had to put up with Cardiff City being the major topic in the Watkins household ever since. It's all your fault dad!*

Carl Dale joined Cardiff City from Chester City in August 1991 and spent seven seasons with the Bluebirds before joining Yeovil Town. He made a total of 253 appearances (212 league) for Cardiff, scoring 94 goals (71 league). Carl is Cardiff's joint 3rd highest goalscorer of all time, alongside Jimmy Gill and behind Len Davies and Robert Earnshaw.

# Foreword by Carl Dale

I originally came to Cardiff on loan from Chester in the summer of 1991 and remember the first time I walked onto the Ninian Park pitch. I felt I was moving to a bigger club and bigger stadium, even though Cardiff were in the fourth division at the time. I think certain grounds have a feel about them and Ninian Park definitely had that. I just felt comfortable there and it was somewhere I knew I wanted to play.

My first game at Ninian Park was against Bournemouth in the League Cup, which we won 3-2 and shortly afterwards I joined on a permanent basis. When I first signed our gates weren't brilliant and playing in front of small crowds didn't help to create an atmosphere. It was completely different though when Ninian was close to full and that happened more frequently as we improved, especially the following season.I experienced good times there, playing in front of big crowds, winning promotion and scoring goals, but I witnessed the downs too when the fans stayed away and I also picked up a few injuries, more than I would like to mention.

The success of the 92/93 promotion season was achieved through a combination of things and as results improved the fans came back in numbers. Players like Robbie James, Phil Stant and Kevin Ratcliffe were added to the squad, which already included the likes of Paul Ramsey and Paul Miller and we had some good youngsters as well in Nathan, Damon and Jason. It was clear we had a strong squad and I think we were always going to do well.

During the promotion season I had a long spell out through injury after snapping my cruciate ligament against Wrexham and that was a low point, even though I was still involved around the team. I'd had a good first season and then scored fifteen goals up to December and I knew there were clubs watching me at the time, but I suppose getting injured meant that I stayed at Cardiff, where I was happy anyway.

I didn't have an operation on my knee until the following summer so it wasn't until midway through the following season that I came back properly. I did a lot of training in the ground itself once I got back to walking and jogging, working with Jimmy Goodfellow. I think I had my own bed in the treatment room and people would come in and visit me, including some of the ex-players and that was part of the experience of spending so much time there.

Harry Parsons always had plenty of stories to tell and he would also take me out across to Bessemer Road market. I thought I was going to end up in hospital a couple of times because of his driving! I would train on the Bob Bank steps and sometimes it was a bit lonely running up and down the terraces on your own, but all that was an incentive to get back playing in front of the fans. I suppose people don't see that side of things, the work you've done to get yourself fit again.

My most memorable goal for Cardiff came in my first game back from injury, ironically against Wrexham in the semi-final of the Welsh Cup, which we went on to win. Although it probably wasn't the best goal I scored for Cardiff, it's the one that sticks in my mind. The thing about it that people didn't realise was that I was actually still injured and I shouldn't have played at all.

I scored that goal with my left foot, which is probably why it went in as I couldn't have hit it that hard with my right. It was quite an emotional moment, because when you've got a serious injury like I had, you're thinking when am I going to get my next goal, how long am I going to be out? But to get back on the pitch from the bench and more or less score with my first touch was fantastic.

I can still remember that moment  and the adrenalin I felt, it's what you play for. The ground was quite full and I ran to the supporters at the Grange End and as I celebrated with them I think the fence nearly came down. All the fans surged forward and the fence actually went through my shirt and my arm got stuck!

Unfortunately things fell apart after the promotion season. Rick Wright had always said that his involvement was only a two year plan and decided to pull out, but there were a few issues behind the scenes which affected certain players and a number of them ended up leaving. I think they would have stayed if there would have been a bit more security as to what was happening within the club. This affected the squad greatly because we were weakened and didn't bring players in.

In the end it took me a couple of years to get fully fit and back to scoring goals again, but to be able to do that after a long period of time out was very satisfying. The team struggled for much of my remaining time at Cardiff and while as a forward it's all about scoring goals, ideally you want to be in a team when your efforts go towards trying to earn promotion. I still enjoyed the seasons when I scored a lot of goals, but I would have preferred us to be at the top of the league rather than the bottom.

As for training facilities at the club, in my time we would go where anyone would let us. It was a combination of working out on the pitch, sometimes the day before the game, doing set pieces and five a side matches, or using Jubilee Park across the road. We also used the astroturf at Sophia Gardens and the university grounds at Treforest. The pitches are certainly a lot better now than they were, but spending time around Ninian Park during the week did make it feel more like home.

I enjoyed playing for Eddie May. As a manager, Eddie was quite laid back. We had a fairly experienced team and although he didn't let us do what we wanted, he knew what he had in place so he put a lot of trust in us. He then came back for a second spell as manager and I remember him asking me to play even though I hadn't really trained, which may not have been a wise thing to do. But because I respected him and as he'd brought me to the club in the first place I went ahead.

I got along with most of my teammates and enjoyed having Jason Perry as a roommate, but as much as he was this hard character on the pitch and used to wind people up all the time, he wasn't at all like that off it. I'm still good friends with Damon Searle, Scott Young, Cohen Griffith – if I don't name them all I'll probably be in trouble! We do still play in the odd game together too, although I struggle to last more than half an hour these days, but then so do the others. On the pitch, I couldn't always understand what Paul Ramsey was shouting to me thanks to his Northern Irish accent, so I would try and keep out of his way, but I had great respect for him as he was our captain at the time.

Unfortunately for me during my time at Cardiff, I didn't score in the bigger games at Ninian Park. Whereas Nathan scored against Manchester City in the FA Cup and Jason scored against Shrewsbury when we got promoted, I got my goals in the bread and butter games when there weren't as many people there. Of course you can't choose your goals, although I'd have liked to have scored more against Swansea! In 1999 I returned to Ninian as a Yeovil player for an FA Cup tie and received a great reception and later that year I was granted a testimonial match against Aston Viilla, which was a very memorable occasion.

I took my son to the last game against Ipswich, which was a sad day. The seats we were sat on were actually moving backwards and forwards so I thought maybe it is now time to change to a new ground! I also played in a charity game at Ninian a few weeks later and ended up scoring the last goal.

I had an affinity with Ninian Park after all the time I'd spent there. When you look back on your career it really should be about what you've won, the games you've played in and the respect you've got from playing, because it soon finishes. You don't forget those memories and my years spent playing at Ninian Park and scoring goals for Cardiff City still stick with me today.

# Introduction

My father first took me to Ninian Park when I was eight years old. It was December 1973 and Cardiff City was a club in decline. Typically though, the Bluebirds treated me to a 4-1 win over FA Cup holders Sunderland, in front of a larger than average holiday crowd. When I say typically, I mean fans are often fooled into thinking they are supporting a great team on their first visit to watch Cardiff play. The truth, of course, is that City almost always disappoint. Being a Bluebirds fan generally tends to be less about the ups and more about the downs.

I don't really remember anything about that first game. The record books say that John Farrington scored a hat trick and Willie Anderson got the other goal as City clinched a big win. I couldn't tell you if we outplayed Sunderland or whether the scoreline flattered us, but what I do remember is Ninian Park itself.

My father took me in the Grandstand and I remember being instantly impressed by the size of the place. I think I spent much of my time watching those around me and taking in what seemed to me to be a vast arena. My thoughts were reinforced when I looked in a football annual I had at home. It listed the capacities of all the stadiums in Britain, with Ninian Park standing fifth from the very top, with room for 62,500 fans. I was already proud to be a Cardiff City fan.

It was a couple of years later that my father began to take me to matches regularly, during the 1975/76 Third Division promotion campaign. After a poor start, Jimmy Andrews and his players shook off the relegation of the previous season and with the likes of Adrian Alston, Tony Evans and Willie Anderson providing the goals and entertainment, City went on a charge up the table. That season, my father would go straight to Ninian Park after he finished work on Saturday morning to pick up two tickets for the Canton Stand and then come home to grab some lunch before taking me off to the ground. The ritual of going to watch Cardiff every other Saturday would soon become engrained in me.

By the time April arrived, the Bluebirds had established themselves in the top three before taking on leaders Hereford United on a Wednesday evening in front of an incredible 35,501 crowd. I can still remember the atmosphere at Ninian Park during that particular game, with people sat in the aisles of the Canton Stand as fans packed into the place. A 2-0 victory helped City to underline their promotion credentials and the runners-up spot was confirmed a couple of weeks later.

The following season, large crowds were commonplace at Ninian, as the likes of Chelsea and Fulham plied their trade alongside the Bluebirds in the Second Division. By that time, we had migrated from our seats in the Canton Stand to the raucous surroundings of the famous Grange End. I would spend my time either perched on a crush barrier, afraid of falling off if my father got carried away with the game and forgot to keep hold of me, or down at the front of the terrace in the Boys Enclosure, leaving my father to shout and curse on his own.

Our FA Cup run during that 1976/77 season still remains vivid in my memory. In particular, the 3-2 win over Wrexham in the fourth round stands out. Almost 29,000 were at Ninian Park for the all-Welsh tie and the fans witnessed a classic encounter in which City took a 2-0 lead through David Giles and Peter Sayer, only for Wrexham to fight back and seemingly snatch a replay when Billy Ashcroft grabbed a last-minute equaliser. However, City weren't finished and John Buchanan sent the home supporters into raptures by firing in an injury-time winner. I'd spent most of the game in the Boys Enclosure and for some reason I'd wiped the Giles goal from my memory, so I thought we'd only earned a draw. Making my way back up to the Grange End, I was happy enough that City had avoided a defeat, only to become happier still when my dad reminded me of the 'forgotten' goal and the fact that we'd won!

Of course, while there were many great Ninian Park moments to savour over the years, there were countless more disappointments. At times, the ground was more a 'Theatre of Nightmares' than a 'Theatre of Dreams' but nevertheless I still loved the old place. During the 36 years I spent visiting Ninian, it changed in appearance quite dramatically and naturally there were many more changes in the 63 years prior to that. Some parts of the ground were redeveloped beyond recognition, while others saw only superficial differences.

The old Grange End, which I stood on as a boy, was demolished in 1978 following the Safety of Sports Grounds Act. Its huge wooden structure was replaced by an open concrete terrace which was much smaller in size and lost to home fans for many years before finally regaining a roof during Sam Hammam's tenure.

The vast Popular Bank, or the Bob Bank as it was better-known, could hold over 24,000 supporters by itself at one stage. Seats were added to the covered section in 1992, but the shape of the stand remained much the same as it had been since the late 1950's.

The Canton Stand, originally built in 1921 with its long wooden benches, remained unchanged until the 1980's, when its capacity was halved as the seats at the rear were removed to make way for executive boxes. Sadly, due to years of under-investment, the boxes were just hollow breeze block shells for twenty years until the work was finally completed in 2001.

The original Grandstand burnt down in 1937. However, until 1973, only the central blocks of the rebuilt Upper Grandstand existed, after which the wings were added. In front of the Grandstand were two enclosures running the full length of the pitch, one situated either side of the players' tunnel. These were initially open terraces and the enclosure closest to the Grange End housed away supporters for much of the late 1970's and throughout the 1980's, after which seats were added in 1991. In later years it was re-branded as the Lower Grandstand – probably only to justify an increase in ticket prices!

During its final year, I photographed Ninian Park at every opportunity, not only at every home game, but also during other events and on non-match days. I found myself taking pictures of the stands, the pitch, the turnstiles, random signs, crumbling concrete, rust and even weeds. I wanted to document Ninian Park in the very last throes of its 99-year existence, warts and all. Now it has gone, all we have are our memories and perhaps these photos to remind us of just how ramshackle but much-loved 'Our Ninian Park' was.

# A Brief History of Ninian Park

by Dave Sugarman

In January 1910, Cardiff City secretary Bartley Wilson attempted to secure an agreement to rent a five-acre patch of land belonging to the Cardiff Corporation, upon which the football club hoped to build a new ground. It was situated between Sloper Road and the Taff Vale Railway Embankment and had previously been used as a rubbish tip, although much of it was being used for allotments at that point in time. Wilson offered the Corporation a rental fee of £60 for the first year, with an annual increase of £10, rising to a maximum of £100. One month later, his offer was accepted by the Parks, Open Spaces and Burial Board Committee on condition that the club provided a number of financial guarantees.

After one of the club's original backers withdrew his patronage, Wilson's plans briefly appeared to be in jeopardy. However, five men soon stepped forward and agreed to act as guarantors. They were Councillors HC Vivian and C Wall, J Bell-Harrison, Lord Rhondda and Lord Ninian Crichton-Stuart. The latter was the second son of the Third Marquis of Bute and although he was never required to put any money into the scheme, his support was nevertheless an enormous boost for the club. The Parks Committee gave the project the green light in April and work on the new ground began within a matter of weeks. The club's directors had originally intended to name it Sloper Park, but they settled upon Ninian Park as a mark of gratitude for Lord Ninian Crichton-Stuart's backing.

Corporation employees, supporters and various other volunteers worked to level the playing area, which they then enclosed with a white picket fence. Low banks of ash and clinker were built up all around the fencing, and a tiny wooden grandstand with a canvas roof, which seated 200 spectators, was erected on the Sloper Road side of the pitch. Dressing rooms were built on the corner of the Canton End along with a small office, and turnstiles were installed at both ends of the ground. Having been laid on the site of an old rubbish dump, the pitch was initially very rough. In fact, the club's first professionals were paid bonuses for removing stones, pieces of glass and other items of debris from the playing surface after their training sessions had finished.

CARDIFF CITY
Association Football Club, Limited.

Opening Match

AT THE NEW GROUND,

NINIAN PARK,

SLOPER ROAD,

Souvenir

Thursday, Sept. 1st,
1910.

v.

Aston Villa

Champions English League 1909-10.

KICK-OFF BY

LORD NINIAN CRICHTON-STUART

AT 5 P.M.

Ninian Park was officially opened on Thursday 1st September 1910, when Football League First Division champions Aston Villa visited Cardiff for a prestigious friendly match. Approximately 7,000 supporters were present as Lord Ninian Crichton-Stuart performed a ceremonial kick-off shortly after five o'clock. A strong Villa side featuring several first-team regulars led 2-0 at the interval, with Walsall-born inside-forward Samson Whittaker having gained the distinction of scoring the first-ever goal at Ninian Park in the eighth minute. City's players gave a much-improved account of themselves during the second half and they managed to reduce the deficit with two minutes remaining. The honour of scoring the Bluebirds' first goal at Ninian fell to Welsh-speaking left winger Jack Evans, who went on to become a legend at the club during an amazing Cardiff City career that spanned no less than sixteen years. The game ended in a 2-1 victory for the visitors, but there was much for the local supporters to be optimistic about on what was a momentous day in the club's history.

Just over a week after the Villa friendly, Scottish centre-half Jack Ramsay netted City's first goal in a competitive match at Ninian Park during a 1-1 draw with Mardy in a Glamorgan League clash watched by a crowd of 5,000. Within a couple of months, construction work began on a much larger grandstand that seated 3,000 spectators upon its completion. The new stand caught the attention of officials from the Football Association of Wales, who awarded Ninian its first international fixture in March 1911. Scotland were the visitors for a Home International Championship match that attracted a gate of almost 17,000 and ended in a 2-2 draw. Sadly, the game was a personal disaster for Scottish captain Peter McWilliam, who badly damaged his knee ligaments on a piece of glass that had worked its way to the surface of the pitch. The injury was so severe that the talented Newcastle United half-back was never able to play professional football again, although he did go on to build a successful career in management with Tottenham Hotspur and Middlesbrough.

Attendances at Ninian Park rose steadily during City's first few seasons as a professional club. In March 1913, a new record crowd of 22,000 packed into the ground to watch the Bluebirds beat Luton Town 3-0 – a victory that secured the Southern League Second Division championship title. The club's directors celebrated its first promotion by commissioning an extension to the grandstand, and by the time the 1913/14 campaign started, it ran the full length of the pitch.

At the end of 1919/20 season, most of the teams in the Southern League's First Division became members of the Football League's newly-formed Third Division. However, Cardiff City were voted straight into the Second Division during a specially-convened meeting of the League's management committee. It was a massive leap forward for the club and the beginning of a golden era that would see Ninian Park play host to some huge crowds.

During the summer of 1920, construction work began on the Canton Stand. It was deliberately built out of alignment with the playing surface as the club originally intended to move the pitch ten yards closer to Sloper Road and build a 9,000-capacity grandstand to replace the one that had been erected ten years earlier. However, a lack of finances meant the plans were eventually shelved, so the Canton Stand sat out of alignment with the pitch for the remainder of the ground's history.

On 30th August 1920, Cardiff's first Football League match at Ninian Park ended in a 0-0 draw with Clapton Orient. Five days later, the Bluebirds defeated Stockport County 3-0, with Birmingham-born centre-forward Arthur Cashmore scoring the first-ever Football League goal at Ninian.

City's average gate during the club's debut season in the Football League was an impressive 29,140. Crowds of over 40,000 were present for Second Division matches against Coventry, Bristol City and Wolves, while the visit of Chelsea in the fourth round of the FA Cup attracted Ninian Park's first 50,000 attendance. The Bluebirds won an exciting tie 1-0 thanks to another Cashmore strike.

Having secured promotion to the top flight at the first time of asking, the club made considerable improvements to Ninian Park during the summer of 1921 at a cost of several thousands of pounds. The ash banking that surrounded most of the field was extended, giving the ground a substantially increased capacity. Building work which had begun a year earlier on the new Canton Stand was completed, and the pitch was re-laid with sea-washed turf. The opening game of the 1921/22 campaign against Tottenham attracted an estimated attendance of 56,000, while the seasonal average rose to 33,340. That figure meant Cardiff were the fifth best-supported side in the country – a position which has subsequently proved to be the club's highest-ever in the national attendance rankings. Only Chelsea, Liverpool, Spurs and Newcastle were watched by bigger crowds.

During the Twenties, some legendary figures graced Ninian Park, including goalkeeper Tom Farquharson, full-backs Jimmy Blair and Jimmy Nelson, half-backs Fred Keenor and Billy Hardy, inside-right Jimmy Gill, and the club's all-time record goalscorer Len Davies. It was far and away City's most successful period in terms of results, the highlights being when the team finished Football League runners-up in 1924, FA Cup runners-up in 1925 and FA Cup winners in 1927.

The next significant change to the ground occurred in September 1928, when the large Grange End stand was opened. The covered wooden terrace housed 18,000 supporters and the team marked its official opening in some style by hammering Burnley 7-0. Scottish striker Hughie Ferguson, who had scored the winner against Arsenal at Wembley in 1927, netted five of the goals as City chalked up a new club record Football League victory.

Although the Bluebirds were on a downward spiral and had been relegated to the Third Division (South) at the end of the previous season, the 1931/32 campaign saw them claim two more club record home wins. In November 1931, non-league Enfield were given an 8-0 thumping in an FA Cup first round tie. The goals were scored by Albert Keating (3), Harry O'Neill (2), George Emmerson (2) and Frank Harris. Then, in February 1932, Thames were crushed 9-2 in a Football League fixture. Welsh international winger Walter Robbins struck five times, while Les Jones, Jim McCambridge, George Emmerson and Albert Keating also netted. Both victories stood as Cardiff's biggest in the respective competitions for the remainder of Ninian Park's history.

The 1933/34 season proved an absolute disaster for the Bluebirds. The team finished rock bottom of the Third Division (South) and crowds at Ninian Park dropped to alarming levels. A new record low attendance of just 2,660 turned out to watch City lose 2-1 to Aldershot in the last-but-one Football League game of the campaign, while less than 1,500 bothered to show up for a Welsh Cup tie against Bristol City.

Having survived a re-election vote in 1934, the club was showing signs of recovery when Ninian Park was severely damaged by a major fire in the early hours of Monday 18th January 1937. City had played Grimsby Town in a third round FA Cup tie on the previous Saturday and it is believed that burglars broke into the club offices in an attempt to steal the takings. It is not known if the fire was started deliberately, but it completely destroyed the wooden grandstand and also killed Jack, the club's watchdog. Fortunately, a black cat named Trixie, who had been the team's lucky mascot at Wembley ten years earlier, managed to escape the blaze. The Grandstand was soon rebuilt in brick and steel, although the new version only extended approximately one third of the pitch length.

Later that year, Racing Club de Lens became the first continental team to visit Ninian Park. A friendly match was arranged by former City defender Johnny Galbraith, who was coaching the French side at the time, and the Bluebirds won it by a 3-1 margin.

In terms of Football League results, the club enjoyed its best-ever season at Ninian Park in 1946/47. A team including such all-time City greats as Alf Sherwood, Billy Baker and Stan Richards romped to the Third Division (South) championship thanks to a brilliant home record which read: played 21, won 18, drawn 3 and lost 0. The 1946/47 season is one of only two in which the Bluebirds have managed to remain unbeaten in every Football League home match.

The club marked its promotion to the Second Division by making a number of alterations to Ninian Park during the summer of 1947. They included building the wall and main gates which stood at the front of the ground, and the installation of two concrete terraced enclosures in front of the main stand.

In November 1949, the Welsh national side recorded their biggest Ninian Park victory when they defeated Belgium 5-1. Aston Villa striker Trevor Ford, who signed for Cardiff four years later, scored a hat-trick, while Manchester City's Roy Clarke and Swansea Town's Roy Paul also found the net.

Speedy centre-forward Wilf Grant was responsible for a couple of astonishing goalscoring records in the early-Fifties. Between March and November 1951, he netted in eleven consecutive Football League games at Ninian Park, scoring seventeen goals in the process. During the 1951/52 campaign, Grant struck twenty seven league and cup goals as the Bluebirds won promotion to the First Division. Amazingly, no less than twenty four of them were scored at Ninian.

In terms of Football League attendances, the 1952/53 season proved the pinnacle for Ninian Park as some huge crowds turned out to watch players such as Dougie Blair, Ken Chisholm and George Edwards in top-flight action. On 22nd April 1953, the club's highest attendance record was set when 57,893 saw the Bluebirds battle out a 0-0 draw with eventual champions Arsenal. The average gate at Ninian during the season was 37,933, which was the largest in Cardiff's history. At that stage, City were the eighth best-supported club in the league.

The Bluebirds set an unwanted club record in September 1955 when they were hammered 9-1 by Wolverhampton Wanderers in a First Division match at Ninian Park. English international winger Johnny Hancocks fired the visitors into a first-minute lead and went on to complete a hat-trick as the men from Molineux ran riot. Centre-forward Roy Swinbourne also bagged a hat-trick, Alf Sherwood scored an own goal and Peter Broadbent netted twice as City were humiliated in front of a 42,546 crowd. Former-Wolves forward Ron Stockin scored a late consolation for the Bluebirds in what was the club's heaviest-ever Football League home defeat.

Later that season, in April 1956, another record was set when 37,500 turned out to watch Cardiff entertain Swansea in the Welsh Cup final at Ninian. City won a thrilling game 3-2 with goals from Brian Walsh (2) and Johnny McSeveney, and the attendance subsequently proved to be the biggest in the history of the competition.

During the 1958 close-season, major improvements were made to Ninian Park's Popular Bank, or the Bob Bank as it was better known. The big terrace was extended in depth, raised in height, the rear sections were stepped in concrete and a roof which ran the length of the pitch was added. The work meant that all four sides of the ground were covered for the first time.

On 17th October 1959, a record Ninian Park crowd assembled to watch Wales take on England in a Home International Championship match. The Welsh team included stars such as Ivor Allchurch, Terry Medwin and Cliff Jones, while the England line-up featured Bobby Charlton, Don Howe and Brian Clough, who was making his international debut. A mammoth gate of 61,556 witnessed a dour contest played in extremely difficult conditions thanks to driving winds and incessant rain. Chelsea striker Jimmy Greaves gave England a half-time lead, but twenty year-old Cardiff forward Graham Moore stole the headlines when he netted a late equaliser on his first appearance for Wales.

Ninian Park was further improved during the summer of 1960 when floodlighting was installed at the ground. Cardiff were one of the last clubs in the Football League to invest in such facilities, but when they finally did arrive they were said to be amongst the very best in the country. The floodlights were officially unveiled when the Bluebirds played a friendly game against Grasshoppers of Zurich in October 1960, although they had already been switched on during a couple of earlier midweek First Division matches against Sheffield Wednesday and Aston Villa.

In January 1961, City recorded their biggest-ever victory in any competition when they slaughtered Knighton 16-0 in a Welsh Cup fifth round tie watched by a crowd of just 3,800. Barry-born forward Derek Tapscott became the first and only player in Ninian Park's history to score six goals during a first team game, while Graham Moore (4), Brian Walsh (2), Peter Donnelly (2), Derek Hogg and Danny Malloy also found the net against the hapless amateurs from Mid-Wales.

Derek Tapscott had the distinction of scoring what proved to be the last-ever top-flight goal at Ninian Park. A dreadful run of form during the second half of the 1961/62 campaign had seen the Bluebirds drop into the First Division relegation zone and they were in desperate trouble by the time West Ham visited South Wales on Easter Monday. Despite their lowly league position, City produced a decent display against the mid-table Hammers and claimed a comfortable 3-0 victory. Striker Dai Ward scored two first half goals and 'Tappy' added a third with a quarter of an hour remaining, but it was a case of too little too late. A disastrous 8-3 defeat at Everton five days later condemned the Bluebirds to relegation and the club never managed to return to the top flight during the remainder of Ninian Park's history.

CARDIFF CITY

SEASON 1970-71

OFFICIAL PROGRAMME

WEDNESDAY, 10th MARCH, 1971
VERSUS
REAL MADRID
KICK-OFF 7.30 p.m.

BLUEBIRDS
1/-
JOURNAL 5p

The 1964/65 season saw Cardiff compete in the European Cup Winners' Cup for the first time and Esbjerg of Denmark were their first opponents in a two-legged preliminary round tie. After a goalless first match, City triumphed 1-0 in the second leg at Ninian, with midfielder Peter King netting the club's first European goal. Surprisingly, the attendance for such a significant fixture was just 8,784.

The Bluebirds recorded their most famous victory in the competition in March 1971, when the mighty Real Madrid were humbled at Ninian Park in a quarter-final first leg tie. A crowd of 47,500 saw the Spanish giants beaten 1-0 by a City side who were top of the Second Division table, thanks to a superb headed effort from centre-forward Brian Clark. Madrid recovered to win a controversial second leg 2-0 at the Bernabeu Stadium, but nothing could detract from Cardiff's achievements a fortnight earlier on what had been one of Ninian's most memorable nights.

A new under-soil drainage system was installed during the summer of 1971, but it initially failed to have the desired effect. The pitch deteriorated dramatically during the 1971/72 season to the point where it became a muddy morass. A huge volume of sand was brought in to make the surface playable, but it didn't do much good and the club received numerous complaints from visiting teams. As a result, more drainage pipework was added and a new pitch was laid once the season had ended. At the same time, work finally began on extensions to the main stand. After fire had destroyed the original Grandstand in 1937, only the centre section had been replaced. The club had intended to extend it shortly after the Second World War, but for various reasons the project failed to get underway until June 1972. When it was eventually finished in July 1973, the Grandstand ran the full length of the pitch, contained almost 5,000 seats and had cost £225,000 to complete.

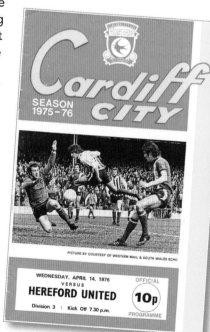

SEASON 1975-76

Cardiff CITY

PICTURE BY COURTESY OF WESTERN MAIL & SOUTH WALES ECHO

WEDNESDAY, APRIL 14, 1976
VERSUS
HEREFORD UNITED
Division 3 : Kick Off 7.30 p.m.

OFFICIAL
10p
PROGRAMME

The Safety of Sports Grounds Act came into being in 1977 and Ninian Park was deemed by the local council to be in such a state of disrepair that it required a number of major structural modifications in order to comply with the new regulations. The club was initially refused a safety certificate before the start of the 1977/78 campaign, but the council eventually relented and allowed City to begin the season with a drastically reduced capacity. A temporary ban on floodlit matches was put in place and the capacity dropped further from 46,000 to just 10,000 while some aspects of the work were being undertaken. The biggest single change to the ground was the demolition of the old wooden stand which had stood at the Grange End since 1928. The roof was removed, the entire structure was dismantled and a smaller open concrete terrace was built in its place. It reopened at the beginning of the 1978/79 season and was given over to away supporters only. By the time all the safety work at Ninian had been completed, it had cost the club a sum of around £600,000. Only a third of that money was provided by the Football Grounds Improvements Trust, while the Football Association of Wales supplied a grant of just £27,000.

The Bluebirds spent much of the next two decades in the bottom two divisions of the Football League. Crowds at Ninian Park hit record lows during the mid-Eighties as the club suffered successive relegations, and City's first-ever season in the Fourth Division was greeted with apathy by the South Wales public. An average gate of just 2,826 for the 1986/87 campaign was the lowest in the club's history, while only 1,334 turned up for the final home game of the season against Hartlepool. That later proved to be the smallest crowd ever to have witnessed a league game at Ninian. Ironically, with so few supporters in attendance, the team put in a fine performance and won 4-0 with goals from Alan Curtis, Jason Gummer, Kevin Bartlett and Paul Wimbleton.

The arrival of Rick Wright as Chairman in 1991 signalled a temporary upturn in the club's fortunes and a number of significant improvements were made to Ninian Park during his brief tenure. Seating was installed in the enclosures at the front of the main stand midway through the 1991/92 season and the area was covered by a roof extension a few months later. Meanwhile, a large section of the Bob Bank terrace was raised and seats were installed along its length in time

15

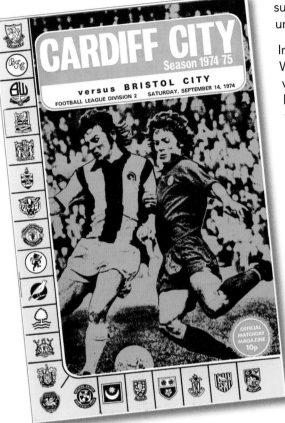

for the start of the 1992/93 campaign, which proved to be a successful one as City won the Third Division championship under the management of Eddie May.

In September 1993, Cardiff played their final European Cup Winners' Cup tie at Ninian Park. The game ended in a 3-1 victory for Belgian visitors Standard Liege, with veteran full-back Robbie James scoring a thunderous 25-yard drive for the Bluebirds. It proved to be the last goal ever scored in a European competition by a Welsh Football League club. Subsequently, a number of League of Wales sides played European Cup Winners' Cup and UEFA Cup matches at Ninian, including Barry Town, Inter CableTel, Cwmbran Town, Haverfordwest County and Carmarthen Town, although none of them even managed to score a goal, let alone win a game.

The last senior international at Ninian was played in March 1998, when Wales drew 0-0 with Jamaica in a friendly fixture watched by a crowd of 13,349. Young Norwich City striker and future Welsh captain Craig Bellamy made his international debut during the second half of an uninspiring game played in torrential rain.

Controversial former-Wimbledon owner Sam Hammam bought Cardiff City in August 2000 and soon announced his intention to move the club to a new 30,000-capacity all-seater stadium. A 62-acre site at Leckwith only a short distance from Ninian Park was identified as being a suitable location for both the stadium and an associated retail development, and plans for the ambitious project were quickly lodged with the local council. However, it would be almost six and a half years before they were granted unconditional status by the authority.

In the meantime, the club made a number of improvements to Ninian. Within weeks of Hammam's arrival, the Grange End was reopened to home fans, although it was divided into three sections so it could be shared with visiting supporters. Soon afterwards, a bar was opened behind the Bob Bank and a big screen was positioned in the gap between the Bob Bank terrace and the Grange End.

The Bluebirds managed to stay unbeaten at Ninian Park for the duration of the 2000/01 campaign as they won promotion to the Second Division. The team's home league record read: played 23, won 16, drawn 7 and lost 0. It was only the second season in which City have remained undefeated in every Football League home match, the first having been back in 1946/47 when the club won the Third Division (South) championship.

Ninian Park was further upgraded during the summer of 2001 when a new roof was positioned over the Grange End. That meant all four sides of the ground were covered for the first time in twenty three years. Other changes included extensive work on the pitch involving the installation of an improved under-soil drainage system, the reopening of the Bob Bank terrace, which had been closed for several years due to safety issues, the building of a bar behind the Grange End and the opening of a new club shop.

After much wrangling with the local council and a takeover deal which saw former-Leeds United supremo Peter Ridsdale replace Sam Hammam as Chairman, work finally began on the club's new stadium project in November 2007. It was estimated the ground would cost somewhere in the region of £46 million to build and would be ready for use in the summer of 2009, meaning the 2008/09 season would be City's last at Ninian Park.

The final FA Cup match at Ninian was played in January 2009, when Cardiff drew 0-0 with Arsenal in front of a sell-out 20,079 crowd. Coincidentally, the Bluebirds had played Arsenal in the final FA Cup game at Highbury three years earlier, shortly before the Gunners relocated to their new home at the Emirates Stadium.

The last-ever Football League match at Ninian Park proved to be a bitter disappointment for everyone involved with Cardiff City. On Saturday 25th April 2009, mid-table Ipswich Town were the visitors for a vital Championship clash as the Bluebirds attempted to secure a place in the promotion play-offs, but they turned in a wretched performance and fell to a dismal 3-0 defeat. Scottish international forward Ross McCormack saw his early penalty saved by Ipswich keeper Richard Wright before Pablo Counago and David Norris struck for Town. The honour of scoring the final goal at Ninian went to Huddersfield-born striker Jon Stead, who netted from close range in the ninetieth minute to set the seal on a thoroughly miserable day for the home fans in a crowd of 19,129.

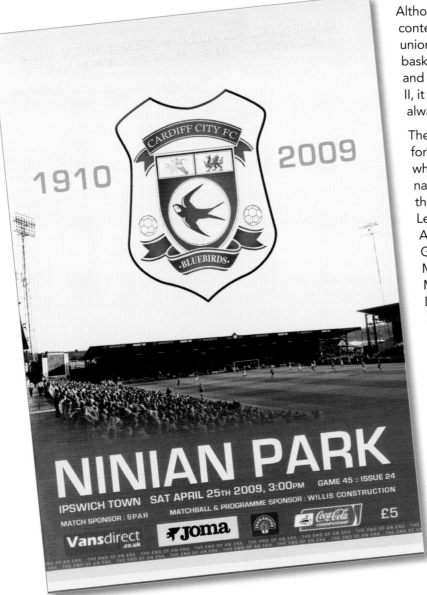

Although the ground hosted boxing contests, rugby league and rugby union matches, show jumping and basketball exhibitions, a pop concert and even a visit from Pope John Paul II, it is for football that Ninian Park will always be best remembered.

The ground was home to Cardiff City for almost one hundred years, during which time some of the biggest names in the British game played there for their clubs and countries. Legends such as Billy Meredith, Alex James, Dixie Dean, Hughie Gallacher, Tom Finney, Stanley Matthews, John Charles, Bobby Moore, George Best and Kenny Dalglish all made appearances at Ninian during the course of its chequered history.

Fans of both the Bluebirds and the Welsh national team experienced numerous highs and lows on Sloper Road over the years, and it's fair to say the bad times often outnumbered the good. Nevertheless, Ninian Park will forever hold a special place in the hearts and minds of the many thousands of players, officials and supporters who visited the famous old ground between 1910 and 2009.

## Chapter 1

# Our Ninian Park

It should have been quite simple to detach ourselves from feeling anything special about what in essence was just a crumbling pile of wood, bricks and concrete for longer than we could remember. However, in reality, Ninian Park was a place where many of us spent a large chunk of our lives over the years, idolising our heroes and berating the less-favoured players in equal measures.

On the big occasions, with the Ninian Park faithful cheering the Bluebirds to momentous victories against the likes of Real Madrid, Tottenham and Leeds, the ground itself seemed to breathe with us, taking in our collective voices and urging the team on by itself. I was too young to go to the Madrid game, but having seen the footage on television, the noise generated when Brian Clark scored THAT goal makes the hairs on the back of my neck stand on end just thinking about it. Listening to BBC commentator Idwal Robling desperately trying to make himself heard as the cameras pan to the massed throngs celebrating on the Bob Bank is truly awe-inspiring.

These are the kind of moments that football fans live for. You somehow put up with all the lows just to get that buzz from the occasional incredible high. I remember how I felt at the Riverside Stadium in March 2008, when Cardiff had beaten Premier League Middlesbrough to reach the semi-final of the FA Cup. The elation of having reached Wembley and the pride in the team's performance helped to make up for the dross served up by numerous Cardiff City teams during much of the previous 35 years I had been watching them.

When it was close to full, Ninian Park was a wonderful place to be. Perhaps in its latter years, after the stadium had shrunk in terms of capacity, its size helped to create a better atmosphere. Of course, the fact that the Bluebirds had re-established themselves in the second tier of the English pyramid system following promotion in 2003 helped to rekindle support for the club, but just imagine if we had still been playing in that 62,500-capacity ground circa 1973. Would the 18,000 fans present for the Burnley home game in April 2009 have managed to generate the same sort of atmosphere with room in the ground for another 44,500 people?

Certainly, for many games during the 1980's and 1990's, we could have made do with just one of the four stands at Ninian Park, as crowds plummeted to record lows. To watch football at Ninian during those dark days was a painful experience and if you pondered on it for too long, it became quite soul-destroying. It's no wonder so many supporters turned their backs on the club. I used to get through the games by trying to introduce some comedy value to the football on offer. Rather than scream and shout at a bad pass or sky-high shot, I would laugh out loud at how inept some of our players were. It probably didn't help matters much, but it did help to get me through it.

Despite the bad times, I was always immensely proud of Ninian Park, right from those early days of being impressed by the sheer size of it. Maybe if I had done a bit more research at the time and discovered that Charlton's ground the Valley had the biggest capacity, then Ninian wouldn't have seemed quite such a magical place. But you don't really choose your football club – it chooses you.

Of course, there were other factors that made Ninian Park that little bit more special than the average Football League ground. It was also a major international venue, hosting most of the big Welsh games until the FAW became strange bedfellows of the WRU in 1989. Indeed, Ninian's biggest-ever crowd of 61,556 was there to witness not a Cardiff City game but a Wales v England fixture in 1959.

So what made Ninian Park special? Being a Bob Banker or a Grange Ender? Maybe it was singing your heart out on the terraces or perhaps it was just the floodlights? Yes, I always loved those floodlights too! There were plenty of older gentlemen in the Grandstand who sat in the same seats for years and rarely uttered a word except for the odd 'get him off' if a player was having a particularly bad game, but I'm sure they loved and sometimes loathed Ninian Park as much as the next man.

The time was probably right for our move to the new stadium and the fact that it is only across the road was perhaps its biggest saving grace. After all, it's not as if we have moved to a junction off the M4 or the other side of Cardiff is it? Aside from that, the club did a magnificent job in delivering a new stadium we can be proud of, but that doesn't mean I don't shed the occasional tear when I think back to our old home.

I suppose I would have liked Ninian Park to have been redeveloped bit by bit, which has happened to some famous old stadiums like Old Trafford and Villa Park, but money dictates these days and the cost of knocking down stands and building them back up would have needed an owner with very deep pockets. The money generated from the sale of the land and the development of the retail units meant the cost of building the new stadium was just a fraction of what staying at Ninian would have been. Sadly, football is all about business these days and we are consumers first, supporters second.

It was a sad moment when the bulldozers moved in only days after Ninian Park had finally closed its doors. The view of the floodlights on the horizon had been a familiar sight for people visiting Cardiff since they were erected in 1960 and it seems strange that they are no longer there. Today, apart from the street names, there is little to suggest that where a modern housing estate now exists, a grand old football stadium stood for some 99 years. These days, people are living in their shiny new homes on the site where we watched the likes of Toshack and Clark, Alston and Evans, Hemmerman and Hatton, Gilligan and Bartlett, Stant and Dale, Thorne and Earnshaw and countless others scoring goals to send the Ninian crowds into raptures. I may have been born in nearby St David's Hospital, but in my heart, along with thousands of others, I was born under a Grange End star.

*Above:* A Packed Ninian Park from the air
– The Bob Bank roof was added in 1958.

*Left:* An aerial shot of Ninian Park, taken in 2004.

*Above:* July 2008 – The Ninian Park pitch ready for action.

*Left:* July 2008 – Ninian Park awaits its final season of football.

*Opposite top:* September 2008 – Fans arrive for the game against promotion favourites Birmingham.

*Opposite middle left:* September 2008 – Heading for the Bob Bank turnstiles.

*Opposite bottom left:* Cardiff fans take heed!

*Opposite bottom right:* Graffiti painted by the main entrance – possibly a declaration of love for Ninian Park?

Ninian Park's floodlights were erected in 1960.

*ve:* More graffiti – Did they run out of paint?

*t:* A weather worn Grandstand turnstile.

*osite top left:* The lettering and Bluebirds were added to the
gates at the start of the 2008/09 season.

*osite top right:* January 2009 – Fans buying souvenirs before
A Cup tie against Arsenal.

*osite bottom:* May 2009 – An end of season collapse robbed
of a play-off match and a final chance to say goodbye.

*Above left:* September 2008 – Fans walking along Sloper Road towards Ninian Park.

*Above right:* The Supporters Club cabin, situated behind the Canton Stand.

*Right:* March 2009 – A view from Jubilee Park.

*Above:* Meeting place for stewards at corner of Canton Stand & Grandstand.

*Top left:* June 2008 – View from the Canton Stand executive boxes.

*Bottom left:* Cash ticket sales booth situated behind the Canton Stand.

THF AREA ABOVE IS COATED WITH NON DRYIN SECUR'TY PAINT.

CARDIFF CITY
These Gates
Will Be
Locked at
5.45pm Daily

*Above:* June 2009 – Shortly before the pitch is torn up for the final time.

*Left:* Gate allowing access to Canton Stand Suites and Bob Bank turnstiles.

*Opposite top left:* Main ticket office at the rear of the Canton Stand – often the scene of much queuing!

*Opposite middle left:* High security at Ninian Park.

*Opposite bottom left:* The souvenir shop – everything must go.

*Opposite top right:* Looking skywards from inside a Ninian Park floodlight.

*Opposite bottom right:* Looking inwards from the main gates.

31

## Chapter 2
# The Bob Bank

When Ninian Park began its existence back in 1910, the Popular Bank was just an ash bank, but looking back at photos from the very early days, you can see the size and shape of what it became. In its heyday, the Popular Bank, dubbed the Bob Bank due to the cost of the entry fee, was a rival to the largest terraces in the country. The Valley, home of Charlton Athletic, and Leeds Road, Huddersfield Town's former ground, both boasted vast open terraces, but the Bob Bank, Ninian Park, came close in terms of size and certainly in atmosphere.

A roof was added in 1958, which gave cover to all but the first few rows of terracing and just two years later, the famous 'Captain Morgan Rum' advert was painted across the roof and remained there for the next 41 years, before finally new sponsors were found, firstly in Hyper-Value and then Brace's Bread. You could cram around 24,000 people onto the Bob Bank before the days of health and safety inspectors. I've stood on the Bob Bank when there was less than half that number and it felt packed, so goodness knows what it was like when it reached near-capacity in the old days.

My earliest memories of the Bob Bank are of a League Cup tie against Queens Park Rangers in 1976. My father would usually take me in the Canton Stand or Grange End, but he must have fancied a change. I remember some sort of deal being cut between him and the turnstile operator and suddenly I was being lifted into the ground. It would have only been about 50p to get me in properly, but my dad had saved a few pence and the turnstile operator had enhanced his match-day wage, so I guess everybody was happy.

*Above left:* May 1972 – A packed Bob Bank watches Wales take on England.

*Above right:* Floodlight at corner of Canton Stand and Bob Bank.

*Opposite:* Looking towards the Bob Bank from the front of the Canton Stand.

I wonder how much revenue the club lost over the years due to that sort of thing? Maybe the reason Cardiff sold John Toshack to Liverpool back in 1970 was due to unscrupulous turnstile operators rather than a lack of ambition from the directors!

By the turn of the 1980's I was going to Ninian Park with my mates and the Bob Bank was our terrace of choice. Crowds were on the wane by then as City continued to struggle, so you had the freedom to stand pretty much where you liked. It was difficult to get any sort of atmosphere going back then with crowds usually dipping below 10,000 and I don't think playing in such a cavernous, empty ground helped the team.

Although I'd been watching City since 1973, it wasn't until 1982 that I realised how much Cardiff City meant to me. We were playing Luton Town at Ninian Park in a must-win game which had attracted a larger than average crowd of 10,277. Defeat against David Pleat's Hatters would consign us to relegation to the Third Division and, with the visitors at the top of the league and heading for the First Division, it was a tough ask. City failed to deliver and went down 3-2, confirming our relegation.

Standing on the Bob Bank at the final whistle I suddenly felt angry and hurt. I suppose I was displaying all the classic emotions of being a teenager, but it felt like I'd fallen in love and been dumped by Cardiff City all on the same night.

The Bob Bank was my home as a City fan throughout the 1980's. Much of the football on display was dire, especially during the Alan Durban era, but I 'kept the faith' as they say, even though many of my mates faded away to do something far more worthwhile and probably entertaining with their lives. Nothing really changed during those years. You'd get wet if you stood at the front, the singing section would do their best to congregate just behind the television gantry, you could get a lukewarm pie and a barely-stirred cup of hot chocolate from the back of the stand while watching the trains go by, and you could use the air-conditioned wall that was loosely described as a toilet if you were really desperate.

Then along came Rick Wright, who in the early 1990's became the first owner to spend any money on Ninian Park for what seemed like years. With the help of a Football Trust grant, he put seats into the Grandstand enclosures and then, in 1992, he raised and seated the covered section of the Bob Bank. I had relocated to the Grandstand by then and no longer being able to see the vast terrace opposite took a bit of getting used to, but I suppose it was a sort of progress.

And that's about it, really. For the next fifteen years or so, nothing else changed on the Bob Bank apart from the odd lick of paint or a new sign appearing and the high metal fences finally coming down. We did, though, eventually get the 'Bob Bank Village' in the area behind the stand which backed onto the railway lines. That was a place where you could get an overpriced pint in less than luxurious surroundings. Still, it was better than what we had been used to, so we were grateful for small mercies.

For me, the best memories of the Bob Bank were when it was still simply one big terrace. It was rarely anywhere near full, but it was the heart and soul of Ninian Park after the old wooden Grange End had been torn down. I loved standing there, often watching the people around me as much as the game itself. Listening to Roxy Music's 'Love Is The Drug' blasting out over the tannoy for the umpteenth time (I think it was one of only three singles the club owned during that period) and grabbing a spot on a favoured crush barrier. When I was on the Bob Bank, it felt like I was at home.

*Opposite top*: April 2009 – City have just beaten Burnley, in what was to be our final victory at Ninian Park.

*Opposite bottom left*: Gangway at the rear of the Bob Bank.

*Opposite bottom right*: Safety gate at front of Bob Bank.

...ve: A sign for very tall people!

...January 2009 – A sold out Bob Bank watch Cardiff earn a replay
...nst Arsenal in the FA Cup.

...t: Originally erected by Sky for a live TV game,
...box was also used to house sponsors and guests.

...osite top: The Bob Bank terrace.

...osite bottom left: Temporary turnstiles for Bob Bank seating
...oter not included

...osite bottom right: April 2009 – The seated area of the Bob Bank,
...to kick off against Swansea.

OTHERS FOLLOW THE TRIBES AND BECOME PART OF THE MASSES,
SOME USE THEIR INSTINCT AND BECOME DISTINCT...........YOU DECIDE

BOB BANK VILLAGE
TOILETS - REFRESHMENTS
- BARS - EXIT

*Above*: Picture of the 1927 FA Cup winning team at side of Bob Bank.

*Right*: The Bob Bank Village provided warm beer and over priced food, but we loved it all the same.

*Opposite:* Seats at rear of Bob Bank, looking towards the disused terracing separating it from the Grange End.

WELCOME TO CARDIFF CITY F.C

Bob Bank Bar

| | | |
|---|---|---|
| Fosters Pint £3.00 | Strongbow Pint £3.00 | John Smiths Pint £3.00 |
| Fosters Half Pint £1.50 | Strongbow Half Pint £1.50 | John Smiths Half Pint £1.50 |
| Soft Drink £1.70 | Lemonade Dash £0.10 | Cordial Dash £0.10 |
| Clark's Pie £2.00 | | Crisps £0.80 |

WATER £1.50

ENJOY YOUR DAY

Bob Bank Burgers

BURGERS, HOT DOGS, HOT AND COLD DRINKS
OTHER FOOD ITEMS AVAILABLE IN THE PIE SHOP

| | |
|---|---|
| | £1.50 |
| Chips | £1.50 |
| Soft Drink | £1.30 |
| Tea | £1.30 |
| Coffee | £1.50 |
| Beef Drink | |

ENJOY YOUR DAY

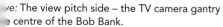

*Above:* The view pitch side – the TV camera gantry in the centre of the Bob Bank.

*Left:* Looking upwards towards the Bob Bank roof.

*Opposite top:* Enjoy your day at the Bob Bank village.

*Opposite bottom:* Overlooking the Bob Bank Village, with Cardiff's main rail depot in the background.

POLITE NOTICE
DO NOT MOVE BETWEEN THE
SEATING AND THE TERRACE
AREAS
YOU MAY BE EVICTED AND
WE LOSE CAPACITY

SAFETY 🚫 NOTICE

To Protect
Lines of Sight
all Umbrella's are
prohibited in
this section
Thank you for your cooperation

CARDIFF
CITY 1

REAL
MADRID 0

*Above:* Approaching the Bob Bank from the Canton End turnstiles.

*Left:* Bob Bank turnstiles – situated at the back of the Canton Stand.

*Opposite left top:* City fans have long been confused by the concept of sitting and standing!

*Opposite left bottom:* Not good news for a wet day on the Bob Bank terrace.

*Opposite right:* Steps at rear of Bob Bank, provided access to refreshments and toilets.

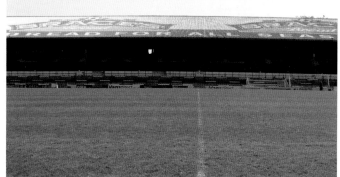

*Above*: June 2009 – Looking across the pitch towards the Bob Bank.

*Top left*: Only the best toilet facilities for Bob Bank customers.

*Top right*: Graffiti at rear of Bob Bank, courtesy of Beefy?

*Bottom left*: Home of St John's Ambulance between Bob Bank and Canton Stand.

*Opposite*: May 2009 – Fans paying their last respects to the Bob Bank at the Open Day.

# Chapter 3
# On the Pitch

If you asked me to name my favourite Ninian Park match, I'd struggle to give you a definitive answer. There have been many great games that perhaps weren't high-profile enough to gain the attention of the media, so therefore have been overlooked.

A game against Plymouth Argyle in August 1986 is one such match. It was Frank Burrows' first season in charge following the disastrous reign of Alan Durban and City were in the Fourth Division for the first time in their history. The Bluebirds had drawn Second Division Plymouth in the first round of the Littlewoods Cup (League Cup) and there was little interest in the first leg, which took place on a blustery autumnal night with just 2,503 in attendance at Ninian Park.

The strong winds gave the visitors a distinct advantage during the first half and they appeared to be out of sight after taking a commanding 4-1 lead, but if ever there was a game of two halves then this was it. City, inspired by diminutive midfielder Nigel Vaughan, embarked on an amazing comeback to win a thrilling contest 5-4. It really was a stunning recovery and the type which I'll probably never witness again. A week later, the Bluebirds completed the job by winning 1-0 at Home Park and they went on to reach the fourth round of the competition before being beaten 1-0 by Shrewsbury Town at Gay Meadow.

I could probably count the games I missed at Ninian Park since the early 1980's on the fingers of one hand, but one match I did miss stands out for many fans as one of their defining memories of Ninian Park. About a week before our FA Cup third round tie against Leeds United in January 2002, I was invited to take part in the Sky Sports Fan Zone programme, which would involve me providing an alternative commentary to Alan Parry and Andy Gray for the live coverage. The downside was that while Gray and Parry would be nestled in the television gantry above the Bob Bank, I would be in a studio in Slough.

It seemed like too good an opportunity to turn down, especially as Sky were offering to pay me £200 just to watch Cardiff City. So on the Sunday morning, after passing my ticket onto my father, I jumped in my car and made the two hour journey along the M4 to the Sky studios. Meanwhile, the South Wales pubs were beginning to fill up with Bluebirds fans and the atmosphere around Ninian Park was building up to electrifying proportions.

I ended up watching one of City's most famous Ninian Park victories in a small darkened room, glued to a large flat screen with a microphone and a Leeds fan for company. It was a surreal experience, but as Cardiff got back into the game after Mark Viduka's early strike, I was immersed in the atmosphere and events as they unfolded. I won't try to pretend that it could ever be as good as actually being at the game, but I can assure you that when Scott Young scored our winner, I was bouncing around the room making my Leeds counterpart feel very uncomfortable!

On the journey home, I tuned into BBC Radio 5 Live, expecting to hear all about our famous victory against a team that were leading the Premier League at the time. What I actually heard was a hatchet job on Cardiff City and Ninian Park, with the reporters intent on concentrating on the negative aspects of the tie, rather than the performance of the team. I'm not one to bury my head in the sand and I know we've had more than our fair share of problems over the years, most of which have been brought about by the conduct of our own supporters, but it seemed that the reaction to our victory over Leeds was one-sided and undeserved.

Perhaps Sam Hammam's biggest mistake on the day was throwing BBC reporter Jonathan Overend out of Ninian Park as he constantly asked questions about the coin throwing and Sam walking around the pitch. This seemed to give the BBC carte blanche to demonise football at Ninian Park and the rest of the media soon jumped on the bandwagon.

I suppose it's always been the cup ties at Ninian that have stood out in the memory, due to the 'winner takes all' fervour that surrounds them, but there have been countless run-of-the-mill league games over the years that have provided equally thrilling entertainment.

The penultimate game at Ninian Park against Burnley on Easter Monday, April 2009, was one such match. City weren't at their best for much of the 90 minutes and Burnley always looked dangerous opponents, but the buzz that you can get from football was encapsulated in those final few minutes after Darren Purse had played a suicidal back-pass to let the visitors equalise. The abject misery and despair felt by all the Bluebirds fans present that day turned to unadulterated joy just seconds later, when Ross McCormack popped up not once, but twice to give us a 3-1 victory. A packed stadium was bouncing and the atmosphere was fantastic. It proved to be the last time that Ninian Park would ever witness such excitement thanks to the dreadful capitulation against Ipswich twelve days later.

*Opposite top:* April 2009 – Cardiff take on rivals Swansea for the final time at Ninian Park.

*Opposite bottom*: Cardiff v Swansea, April 2009 – City players celebrate Michael Chopra's goal in front of the Canton Stand.

*Above:* Cardiff v Swansea, April 2009 – And the Bob Bank goes wild!

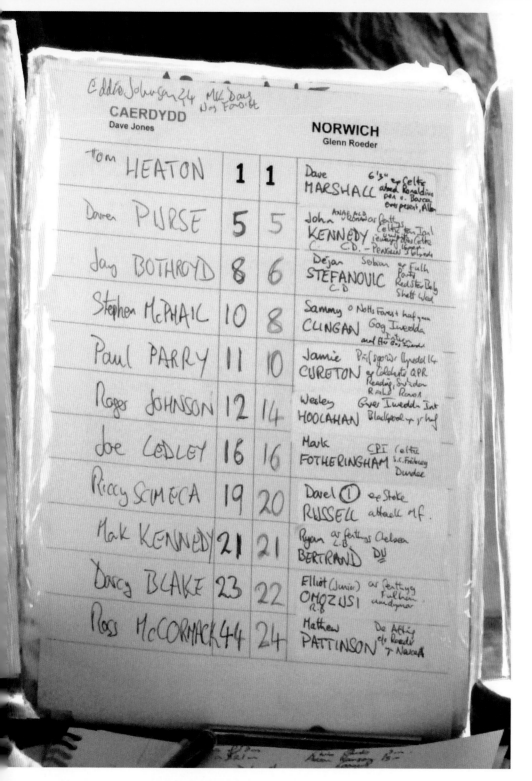

*Left:* August 2008 – Notes for the media guys, David Marshall in goal for Norwich.

*Opposite top:* Night games at Ninian Park have always been special, this one against Barnsley was one of the last.

*Opposite bottom:* March 2009 – On-loan Eddie Johnson finally hits the net against Doncaster amid wild celebrations.

*Above*: September 2008 – Some fans enjoying an after match pint in the Grandstand bar.

*Opposite far right top*: October 2008 – City legend Phil Dwyer at Ninian Park with his grandchild.

*Opposite far right bottom*: March 2009 – Cardiff born Joe Ledley captains the Bluebirds against Doncaster.

*Opposite right*: January 2009 – Wayne Routledge's decision to snub City for QPR makes the back page headlines.

*Above:* September 2008 – City stewards await the arrival of the Grange Enders.

*Opposite bottom:* October 2008 – Roger Johnson gets a tackle in against Charlton.

*Opposite top:* January 2009 – Souvenir sellers on Sloper Road, with the new stadium taking shape a short distance away.

*Above*: March 2009 – Cardiff prepare to take on Sheff Utd in a vital game against play-off rivals.

*Opposite top*: November 2008 – Peter Whittingham aims for goal against Crystal Palace.

*Opposite bottom left*: Has the Echo seller had a sneaky pint?

*Opposite bottom right*: October 2008 – Charlton's Mark Hudson gets a straight red card, the following season he joined Cardiff.

*Opposite:* January 2009 – A sell out crowd hopes for an FA Cup upset.

*Above:* January 2009 – Arsenal manager Arsene Wenger looks concerned as Cardiff make a real game of it.

*Top right:* January 2009 – City and Arsenal take to the field for what turned out to be the last FA Cup game at Ninian Park.

*Bottom right:* January 2009 – Arsenal fans were allocated the entire Grange End due to FA Cup ticketing rules.

*Above:* September 2008 – Outside the main gates.

*Opposite top left:* August 2008 – City begin their last season at Ninian Park against Southampton.

*Opposite bottom left:* December 2008 – The floodlights are switched on early for the Christmas holiday game against Plymouth.

*Opposite right:* August 2008 – Steve Thompson was in the line up, before moving to Burnley.

POLITE NOTICE
DO NOT MOVE BETWEEN THE
SEATING AND THE TERRACE
AREAS
YOU MAY BE EVICTED AND
WE LOSE CAPACITY

*Above:* April 2009 – Cardiff & Burnley players shake hands before a pulsating match.

*Opposite:* April 2009 – Fans celebrate Ross McCormack's late winner, but it was Burnley who went on to the Premier League.

*Left:* April 2009 – Clean up time after the Burnley game, with just one more league game to come at Ninian Park.

*Above:* September 2008 – View from the Grandstand as City take on Birmingham.

*Right:* September 2008 – Fans snap up souvenirs after the local derby against Bristol City.

*Top left*: September 2008 – A handy shelf for your empty bottles & cans.

*Top right*: April 2009 – Not my idea of an office.

*Left*: March 2009 – Disaster strikes as ref Paul Taylor send off two City players and Sheff Utd cruise to a 3-0 win.

## Chapter 4
# The Grandstand

My treat as an eight year-old boy was a seat in the Grandstand for my first ever game at Ninian Park, but it was obviously an expensive one as my father never took me in there again and chose the cheaper option of the Canton Stand or Grange End for future visits. Apart from the odd charity or friendly match, when the rest of the ground remained closed, I don't think I watched another game from the Grandstand for nearly twenty years. After all, it was full of old blokes wasn't it – never really the place to go for an atmosphere.

The original Grandstand was built in 1910 and was a simple wooden structure with a canvas roof and room for just 200 supporters. Within a year of Ninian Park's existence, a more permanent structure had been built and by 1913 it stretched the full width of the pitch with standing room in front. However, the other three sections of the ground were no more than open banks with simple fencing separating fans from the playing area.

The lettering above the centre section was partially obscured after the roof extension was added.

In January 1937, a fire completely destroyed the Grandstand. Thieves were suspected of being responsible, with takings from the previous weekend's FA Cup tie against Grimsby being their likely target. The money wasn't even on the premises, but the damage had been done and for the next year, temporary changing rooms were used behind the Canton Stand to allow matches to continue. By 1938, a new Grandstand had been built. It was a brick and steel structure, but it only spanned the centre section of the pitch, with full length terraced enclosures added in front of it shortly after the Second World War.

The Grandstand as we came to know it was completed in 1973, with the wings being added to the existing structure just a few months before my first visit and its wooden seats remaining until my very last. In 1991, the enclosures below the Grandstand were fitted with blue plastic seats and unveiled for the home match against Maidstone on New Years Day 1992 before a bumper crowd of 8,023, which was more than double what we were usually getting back then. How many times have we seen City freeze in front of a larger than average crowd? The Bluebirds duly obliged as centre half John Williams got himself sent off and the team fell to a humiliating 5-0 defeat.

It was around that time that I said my farewells to the Bob Bank, which I considered my spiritual Ninian Park home, and took a seat in the Grandstand. By now, with City continuing to flounder, most of my mates had got married, had kids or found better things to waste their money on and I'd got involved with the Supporters Club, so it made sense to make the move and sit with them.

The atmosphere was also changing in the Grandstand. Away fans were situated in Block A, whilst groups of City lads were now making the transition from the terraces, which were swiftly being replaced by seats, to Block F of the Grandstand. Sitting between Blocks B and E during those years, you were surrounded by noise and banter, although there were still plenty of the old guys ready to give you a discerning look if you dared to join in.

One of the most infamous moments in the Grandstand's history was of course the trouble at the game against Swansea in December 1993. A large group of Swansea fans, arriving at the ground late, were intent on causing havoc in an already heated atmosphere. Some of the old wooden seats were ripped up and thrown towards the family section seated below in the old enclosures. People in blocks B and C of the Grandstand panicked, causing mayhem by the exits as stewards tried to clear the area and by now seats were flying everywhere as they were returned to where they came from by the adults (and possibly some of the kids) in the family section.

There was a pitch invasion as City fans streamed out of the Bob Bank and for a few minutes all hell seemed to break loose. Eventually, the police regained control and the match went ahead, but once again Ninian Park was in the national headlines for all the wrong reasons. Despite the fact that Swansea fans had clearly been the instigators on this occasion, Cardiff supporters were equally condemned by the media.

It was a defining moment because for a number of years a complete ban on away fans was instigated whenever Cardiff played Swansea and then coach-only 'bubble' trips became the norm.

In later years, away fans were re-housed in a section of the Grange End, leaving the City lads to relocate from Block F to Block A and the lower section below. During its last few years, the atmosphere in at least one side of the Grandstand was as good as anywhere else in the ground, although there were still a few fans who seemed content to spend the entire 90 minutes watching their opposite numbers rather than the game itself. There was a time when perhaps glaring at opposition supporters was more entertaining than watching the match, but the football had improved significantly since our return to the Championship!

After spells in blocks B and E and even a season back on the Bob Bank, I settled into my seat in Block C, close to the Director's Box and near the halfway line. For all its faults and sometimes a lack of atmosphere, the view of the game from the Ninian Park Grandstand was second to none. I miss the wooden seats, the complete lack of clarity from the tannoy (even though Ali Yassine was sitting just a few yards away in his PA box) and the narrow bars underneath, which were a nightmare to get served in. As for my actual seat, well I won't miss that at all, as it's now sitting proudly in my garden. I consider it my little piece of the Grandstand, mine to sit on and reminisce for many years to come.

*Above:* May 1972 – A packed Grandstand, before the wings were added, watch Wales take on England.

*Opposite top:* The Grandstand in June 2008 – The lower section seats and front roof extension were added in 1991/92.

*Opposite bottom left:* Upper and Lower Grandstand turnstiles.

*Opposite bottom right:* Wooden seats in the Upper Grandstand.

*Above:* The Players Bar in the Upper Grandstand was actually more of a corridor!

*Left:* Cardiff's PA Announcer Ali Yassine, ready for action in his box at the back of Block C of the Grandstand.

*Opposite top:* Looking upwards to the Grandstand from pitchside.

*Opposite bottom left:* April 2009 – A packed Grandstand watch City take on Burnley.

*Opposite bottom right:* Advice for supporters in the Lower Grandstand – did anyone ever see a customer services steward?

*Above:* The away dugout in front of the Grandstand.

*Right:* Many of the Grandstand faithful chose to head for this early in times gone by.

*Above:* Padded seats were only added to the directors' box area in later years.

*Left:* Note the no smoking signs – the original Grandstand was destroyed by fire in 1937.

*Above:* Refreshment areas in the Grandstand were somewhat basic, much like the rest of Ninian Park.

*Top:* They even had arm rests in the Directors' Box!

*Right:* Moving advertising panels, added to the front of the Grandstand as City attempted to move with the times.

*Opposite:* The roof extension provided fans in the lower Grandstand with at least some protection from the elements.

*...ove:* May 2009 – Many of these seats were bought by ... at the end of the season.

*...ht:* May 2009 – Shortly before my own Upper ...ndstand seat was removed, it now resides in my ...den.

*...osite far left:* Upper Grandstand litter, waiting to be ...red after a home game.

*...osite top right:* Weather worn plastic seats in the ...er Grandstand.

*...osite bottom right:* Safety gate at the front of the ...ndstand.

## Chapter 5
# Ninian Events

Over the years, Ninian Park hosted many different events, some bizarre and some less so. On the pitch we had boxing, show jumping and a Bob Marley concert to name but a few. In 1982, Pope John Paul II packed out the place on his visit to Cardiff, but chants of 'Bluebirds' were apparently few and far between. In the 1990's, the Jehovah's Witnesses used to hold an annual event at Ninian

*Above:* June 1982 – Pope John Paul II packs in the crowds at Ninian Park.

*Opposite:* July 2008 – The Canton Suite prepares for its last ever wedding.

Park. They were given use of the stadium for free and in return they would give it a new lick of paint.

For most of the time though, Ninian Park stood unused and unloved apart from on match days. The old Bluebirds Club, situated at the junction of the Canton Stand and Bob Bank, was often used for social gatherings but closed in the early 1980's. Despite a brief attempt to resurrect it a few years later, it soon fell into disrepair and was finally demolished.

Inside Ninian Park, there was very little space for the few facilities that existed. The bars were small and pokey and even the Boardroom and Directors Box area, later to be renamed the John Charles Suite, were suitable only for small gatherings or meetings.

Finally, when Sam Hammam came to the club in 2000, work began on completing the eyesore above the Canton Stand which was the row of empty concrete shells that had stood open to the elements for nearly twenty years. The Canton Suite was born and suddenly there was a decent-sized space available to entertain guests and provide something closer to the corporate experience many other clubs could offer.

Around the same time, the law changed to allow civil marriage ceremonies to take place at designated venues and soon afterwards Ninian Park was granted a license. Some people dream of getting married in a big church, others in a castle or a stately home, but for some Ninian Park seemed to make perfect sense.

It was, after all, the closest thing many of us had to a church, a place where we would congregate to sing and worship. And, of course, you got the chance to have your wedding photos taken on the hallowed turf.

In July 2008, I was asked by an old school friend if I would be the official photographer at his wedding, which was to be held at Ninian Park. Of course, I jumped at the chance and it turned out to be the very last wedding at Ninian. On Saturday 12 July 2008, Steven Smith (known to many City fans as Beany) married Mandi Smith. It was a wedding with a difference, as both the bride and groom wore black with a hint of purple. Those of you who have met Beany will know that he and his partner were never likely to have a conventional wedding.

It really was a great day. I photographed the bride and groom and their families and friends in the stands and on the pitch, people did the 'Ayatollah' and then we settled back in the Canton Suite to eat and listen to the speeches. In the evening, the disc jockey, another Bluebirds fan, blasted out City-related tunes as well as a healthy smattering of ska and punk classics. It was certainly a day never to be forgotten.

*Above:* Sharing a kiss on the Ninian Park pitch.

*Opposite top:* The Groom, 'Beany' (right) & guests arrive for a somewhat unconventional wedding.

*Opposite bottom left:* Is it time to 'Do The Ayatollah' yet?

*Opposite bottom right:* Stephen & Mandi exchange rings.

*Above:* In front of the players tunnel with City's Chief Safety Officer Jeff Richards, who sadly passed away in 2009.

*Top:* Group photos in the Canton Stand.

*Right:* Cutting the cake, adorned with Cardiff City badges and Living Dead Dolls!

During Ninian Park's final year, there were numerous other off-field events such as book launches, the children's Christmas party, which is organised each year by the Supporters Club, and finally the hastily-arranged 'Party in the Park' after the team had spectacularly blown their play-off chances.

Football being the business it is today, Ninian Park was never really able to fulfil the requirements of its investors to constantly generate cash. Its facilities were poor and under-used. With the move to the new stadium, the club has been able to generate tens of thousands of pounds of additional income by utilising its 700-capacity restaurant and various other corporate rooms for events and conferences. With Cardiff's football and rugby teams both making use of the stadium, the turnover has vastly exceeded what was possible at Ninian Park.

Ninian events were always rough and ready, take 'em or leave 'em affairs. If you were a guest on a match day as a match or ball sponsor, you would never expect to be treated like royalty. Realistically, it was more a case of a Clark's pie and a Welsh cake at half-time and then you would be required to buy your own beer. After the game, when the girls serving behind the bar wanted to go home, they would tell you in no uncertain terms to get out. To be honest, most of us were used to being treated like that and in reality Ninian Park was never in any danger of being taken over by the prawn sandwich brigade.

*Left:* December 2008 – Setting up for the Children's Christmas Party in the Canton Suite.

*Opposite top:* Supporters young and not-so-young tucking into the party food.

*Opposite bottom:* The players arrive – Gavin Rae signing this young City fan's shirt.

*Above:* And smiling for the camera!

*Above:* Peter Whittingham gaining some new admirers.

*Right:* Kevin McNaughton with a shy supporter.

*Opposite left:* City Kid also joins in the festive fun.

*Opposite top right:* Eddie Johnson signs a ball.

*Opposite bottom right:* Santa arrives 'Doing The Ayatollah'.

MERRY CHRISTMAS TO ALL OF OUR VISITORS
FROM THE GRANDSTAND LADIES' TOILET
COMMITTEE

ENJOY YOUR LAST CHRISTMAS IN OUR
WONDERFUL 5* FACILITY.

*Opposite:* Jay Bothroyd joins in with the party games.

*Above:* Not many people knew of the 'Grandstand Ladies Toilet Commitee'.

*Below:* They made the most of their modest area.

*Top right:* What else went on behind closed doors I wonder?

*Bottom right:* And even Santa was asked to pop in!

*Above:* The Player of the Year evening was held at the SWALEC
Stadium immediately after the Ipswich debacle.

*Opposite:* Whilst Roger Johnson is named Player of the Year.

## Chapter 6
# The Grange End

I was born under a Grange End star, or so the song goes. I think everybody who started watching City in the 1960's or 1970's has a special affinity with the Grange End. After all, it was our home end wasn't it? The Bob Bank had its moments, but there were times when the away supporters were situated on that terrace and just about everywhere else at Ninian Park at one point or another. However, until the old wooden structure was knocked down in 1978, the Grange End belonged exclusively to Cardiff City fans, although in the early 1970's there were several attempts by away supporters to take it over.

*Above:* May 1972 – Supporters in the old wooden Grange End watch as England attack the Canton End.

The Grangetown End, so-named due to the district of Cardiff it was closest to, was opened in 1928, the funds from City's FA Cup triumph the previous year helping to pay for it. Previously just an open ash bank, the new structure was a stepped wooden terrace holding 18,000 spectators. It originally had a basic flat roof which was replaced just a couple of years later by a more conventional pitched roof.

I spent much of the 1976/77 season watching City from the Grange End. I was only eleven going on twelve, so would sit on a crush barrier alongside my dad to get a decent view. Crowds were reasonably healthy during that season and we had several attendances of over 20,000 and even one of over 35,000 for the visit of Everton in the fifth round of the FA Cup. The noise generated from the Grange End was impressive, especially to an eleven year-old kid, but I used to spend much of my time grabbing hold of my father and reminding him to hang onto me whenever he started to get too involved in the game.

When he wasn't forgetting to keep hold of me, he would be blowing cigarette smoke in my face or shouting 'C'mon City' at the top of his voice and right into my ear. It was no wonder I used to disappear to the Boys Enclosure at the front of the Grange End. I suppose it was also no wonder that the place was condemned just a couple of years later following the Safety at Sports Grounds Act. The amount of people smoking and subsequently dropping their cigarette ends onto the wooden floor below must have been an accident waiting to happen when you think about it.

The Grange End back then was considerably larger than it was after it was rebuilt. It used to extend all the way back to the wall which later became a walkway at the rear. I remember the entrance and exits to the Grange End being in the middle of the terrace, taking you underneath the structure to the gates and turnstiles.

When the original Grange End was condemned, other parts of the stadium were also hit with restrictions and the ground capacity was severely reduced. After it was demolished in 1978, the old stand was replaced by a bland open terrace. It may have still been called the Grange End, but the new concrete structure was soulless and typical of the lack of ambition shown by the club's directors at the time. A part of Ninian Park died the day the old Grange End was torn down, that's for sure.

The City fans that were left now stood on the Bob Bank, with the new Grange End being given over to the away fans when it became clear nobody wanted to stand on it. The away fans couldn't get an atmosphere going on it either, so the whole of Ninian Park suffered. Without a noisy away following, there was little

*Above:* The Grange End in May 2009 – Seats were added to the front of the visitors section only a few years previous.

*Right:* Grange End home turnstiles.

*Opposite right:* And from the inside.

incentive for the home fans to sing, not that we actually had much to sing about as the club flirted with liquidation and the team slipped further down the Football League.

The Grange End got a new lease of life in the 1990's when Rick Wright bought out Tony Clemo. During the 1992/93 promotion campaign, it was once again somewhere near full, with a new generation of City fans cheering on 'Eddie May's Barmy Army' and the away fans relocated to the Grandstand. There were problems though, with some of the younger fans trying to mimic the antics of the Grange Enders of the past. Missiles were thrown on more than one occasion and restrictions or complete closure was threatened by the authorities.

Despite its rebirth, the Grange End still missed that special something and it wasn't until the turn of the century that we saw Ninian Park once again look complete when Sam Hammam invested in a roof in 2001 and recreated the atmosphere of old once more. There were concessions though, as the Grange End was divided into three sections – a quarter for the away fans in the corner closest to the Grandstand, another quarter as a no-go zone and finally the remaining half for the City fans.

A whole generation of Grange Enders were lost during those barren years in the 1980's, but as Ninian Park neared its finale, they were back. The new generation were almost as strong in voice as their predecessors and just as troublesome on occasions, but once more the famous old terrace had become a part and parcel of the Ninian Park experience. Keep off the Grange End!

*Above:* April 2009 – Burnley fans in the away section, despite losing that day, they went on to win the Play-Offs.

*Opposite top right:* The Grange End terrace, where many young City fans were nurtured.

*Opposite top left:* Exit gates onto Sloper Road, with the new stadium in the background.

*Opposite middle left:* Looking across the Grange End from the corner of the Bob Bank.

*Opposite bottom left:* March 2009 – Looking towards the Grange End from the Bob Bank as City take on Watford.

*Opposite bottom right:* Ticket booths on Sloper road.

*Above:* Exit steps at the rear of the Grange End.

*Top right:* Limited refreshment facilities at the rear.

*Middle right:* Away supporters had the option of seats in the front section of the Grange End.

*Right:* Away supporters turnstiles.

IT IS AN OFFENCE TO ENTER THE FIELD OF PLAY OFFENDERS WILL BE **ARRESTED**

# CARDIFF CITY FC

## Notice to spectators and staff

### Beware of footballs entering the spectator areas

*Above*: Grange End toilets – a reminder why drinking too much in the ground was not always a good thing.

*Top left*: Pitch invaders were few and far between in the latter years.

*Middle Left*: Surely only a sign to keep the health & saftey officers happy?

*Bottom left*: Refreshment facilities for away fans were no better either.

*Above:* Grange End seating for away supporters.

*Right:* May 2009 – Soon the Grange End terrace would be ruduced to rubble.

*Opposite top left:* The initial structure of the new stadium is just visible between the Grange End and Grandstand.

*Opposite bottom left:* May 2009 – A weather worn sign from the Bob Bank that had found it's way to the Grange End.

*Opposite right:* May 2009 – A few supporters play homage to the Grange End.

PLEASE ASK
CUSTOMER SERVICES
STEWARD
IF ANY ASSISTANCE
IS REQUIRED

P LI E NOTICE
DO NOT MOVE BETWEEN THE
SEATING AND THE TERRACE
AREAS
YOU MAY BE EVICTED AND
WE LOSE CAPACITY

# Chapter 7
# Inside Ninian Park

Aside from the Grandstand, there wasn't really a lot else going on under the other stands at Ninian Park. The Bob Bank and Grange End were pretty much how you saw them. There was nothing hidden going on. No secret underground walkways or bunkers. Apart from the odd toilet and storeroom, what you saw was what you got.

Of course, the Canton Stand did hold a little more interest once the executive boxes and lounges (I use those terms very loosely) were completed, while the ticket office at the back of the Canton was once the Supporters Club shop in the mid 1990's. At the time, with the decaying unfinished boxes above, the area resembled a bomb site rather than a place for fans to gather. The roof leaked, the floor leaked and I think even the walls leaked.

Thankfully, after some much-needed investment by Sam Hammam (investment that later turned out to be more debt), the place was given an overhaul. The Supporters Club were swiftly evicted from their office and moved into a leaky portakabin (well, we were used to it) and the girls in the ticket office never had to experience any damp conditions as the space above was finally completed and the Canton Suite and International Lounge were born. Additional office space was also added for the club's commercial arm.

However, it was the Grandstand that remained the real hub of the Football Club until its final days. Most of that area was considered out of bounds to the average supporter, although if you were willing to queue for long enough at one of the open days, you could at least get to see some of what went on behind closed doors.

The main reception area didn't change a lot over the years. It may have had a lick of paint and some funky furniture added, but in essence it was just a space under the stairs that took you up to the Boardroom. The porch was added in the 1990's, a bit of double glazing to protect the office staff from the elements, but it was still very much the same as when the new Grandstand was built in 1938.

*Above:* Framed photographs of teams from yesteryear adorned the walls.

*Left:* The main entrance into Ninian Park.

*Below:* Stairs leading from reception to the Board Room and John Charles Suite.

Inside, seldom-used offices and storage areas were converted into dining rooms as Cardiff City Football Club was dragged kicking and screaming into the modern corporate age. For a few hundred pounds you could enjoy a day out at Ninian Park with some friends, spend time in the company of ex-City players such as Roger Gibbins and the late Ronnie Bird, have a meal and a few beers and maybe even get to take home the match ball or a framed match programme. It wasn't great, but to be fair to those involved, they did their best to make the most of the humble surroundings.

Further inside were the manager's office, the referee's room and the changing areas. I'm not sure if cups of tea were ever hurled around Ninian's inner sanctum, but it felt magical to take a peek there. It was a kind of forbidden pleasure. I was lucky enough to play at Ninian Park once in a Supporters Club match. It was a real thrill to use the changing rooms and run down the tunnel onto the pitch.

Despite the amount of activity that went on inside the lower section of the Grandstand, you always had the impression that space was at a premium, with office staff, commercial staff and playing staff constantly vying for extra room. In later years, portakabins were added around the perimeter of the ground to house additional employees as departments outgrew their limited areas.

*Left:* Limited office space at the rear of the Canton Stand.

*Middle:* Space was at a premium at Ninian Park.

*Right:* Exit doors from John Charles Suite to Grandstand seating areas.

*Above:* Trophy cabinet in the John Charles Suite.

*Far left:* A Welsh dragon lurking in the corridors.

*Left:* Heading towards the tunnel.

*Opposite:* The John Charles Suite.

A trip up the winding staircase above the reception area would take you to the John Charles Suite on the right and the Boardroom on the left. Neither was spacious, but both served a purpose. The trophy cabinet in the John Charles Suite hinted at former glories, with pennants exchanged during European Cup Winners Cup excursions and international caps from past players on display.

Outside of these rooms were the public areas, accessed by those in the Upper Grandstand. A narrow bar served blocks A, B and C and a similar structure on the opposite side catered for blocks D, E and F. Apart from the obligatory snack bars and toilets that had seen better days, that was about it. Underneath, bars and food areas were added just a few years before the ground closed in order to serve fans in the Lower Grandstand areas, where previously a lukewarm cup of tea was about all that was on offer.

When you consider the space that is now available underneath the stands of the new stadium, it's hard to believe that Cardiff City continued to operate in such a confined area. If Ninian Park had been redeveloped, I suppose the front of the Grandstand could have been extended, maybe almost out onto the pavement of Sloper Road. After all, there are many other stadiums in the country that have similar set-ups.

In the end, the financial pull of building from scratch proved too much and Ninian Park was considered inadequate for a modern day football club. Having been inside most of the ground, I can fully sympathise with that viewpoint, but however pokey it may have been, it still felt like a mysterious unknown world whenever you stepped inside Ninian's inner sanctum.

*Above:* Team bath/shower room.

*Left:* The home changing room.

*Opposite:* The Boardroom.

109

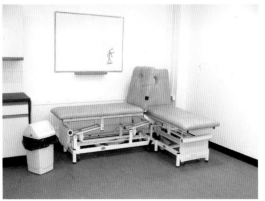

*Above:* Bar area in the Canton Suite.

*Far left:* The rather basic treatment room.

*Left:* Ninian Park art on display during a book launch in the Canton Suite.

*Opposite:* Programmes and old photographs on display.

## Chapter 8

# The Canton Stand

As a kid, I used to love the Canton Stand. My father would go to the ground on Saturday lunchtime to collect our tickets – I think you had to buy them before 1pm to get a discount for children – and then, after some lunch, we would make our way to Ninian Park. At the time we lived in Pontcanna, but my father would usually take the short drive to Canton and park up somewhere near the shopping area.

We'd always try to get seats near the back to get a better view. When I say seats, the Canton Stand was actually populated by long wooden benches, with lines painted across them every couple of feet to separate them into individual seats. There were no backs to the benches, but that didn't matter to me. Just being behind the goal, especially when City were attacking, was a great thrill.

*Above:* Derek Showers celebrates a goal in front of the Canton Stand.

At that time, the Canton Stand was probably twice as deep as it ended up, so the view from the back rows was quite good. After my childhood days on the Canton Stand and then Grange End, I've never particularly enjoyed watching games from behind the goal, but back then it was great to see the players in close-up whenever there was an attack being launched or a corner to defend.

The memory of a packed Canton Stand and indeed a packed Ninian Park when City attracted a crowd of over 35,000 for the famous midweek fixture against Hereford stays with me even today. Imagine that – 35,000 people to watch the Bluebirds play Hereford. Amazing!

The Canton Stand was the oldest existing stand at Ninian Park when the ground closed and, like the Grangetown End, it was named after the district of Cardiff it backed onto. Originally built in 1920 to coincide with City's election to the Football League, its wooden benches could seat around 5,500 fans. Despite the fact that the Canton Stand and Grandstand were the only structures at Ninian Park at that time, an estimated crowd of 50,000 attended the fourth round FA Cup tie against Chelsea in March 1921. The open banks of the Bob Bank and Grange End provided space for tens of thousands of additional supporters.

*Above:* The Canton Stand in its final year.

*Above:* The rear of the Canton Stand.

At the beginning of the 1980's, the Canton Stand, along with many other areas of the ground, took a turn for the worse. The plan was to remove the rear rows of seats and replace them with a tier of executive boxes. The concrete structures were completed, but then the club ran out of money and the open breeze block boxes stood at the mercy of the elements for twenty years. Only at Cardiff City!

Rick Wright replaced the wooden benches with blue plastic seats in the 1990's and finally the executive boxes were completed in 2001. For most of its existence in modern times, the Canton Stand attracted a family crowd, even when it wasn't designated as a family stand. It was always too far from the away fans to be much of an attraction for groups of lads, although it did have its moments over the years. Remember the games against Chelsea and Sheffield Wednesday during the 1983/84 season? Fans of both clubs came to Ninian Park in their thousands as they chased promotion to the First Division. City fans on the Bob Bank were almost surrounded, although the old timers in the Grandstand weren't going anywhere!

The Chelsea game in particular was quite comical. With the Bluebirds leading 3-0, hundreds of visiting fans left Ninian Park early, probably to organise some sort of post-match ambush. Then, thanks to the City players losing their nerve and the referee losing his bottle in a hostile atmosphere, Chelsea came back strongly and had a chance to equalise from the penalty spot in the dying seconds. Suddenly, hordes of visiting supporters were streaming back into the stadium at the junction of the Canton Stand and Grandstand. Chelsea duly scored to make it 3-3 and mayhem ensued outside the ground after the match.

If you looked at the Canton Stand from the Grange End, the stand was noticeably lopsided. The left-hand side began in line with the Grandstand, while the right hand side finished inside the edge of the pitch and some distance from the Bob Bank. Back when the Canton Stand was initially constructed, the plan was to rebuild the Grandstand closer to Sloper Road and also to move the pitch, but for some reason that never materialised, leaving the Canton Stand forever out of line with the rest of Ninian Park.

I think the Canton Stand was spoilt when they took out the rear rows of seats, and I never watched a game from there again after that, but it was a great place to follow City as a kid and I'm sure there are countless more Bluebirds who began their time watching Cardiff City from there.

*Below:* Canton stand turnstiles.

*Above:* View from a Canton Stand executive box.

*Left:* Looking towards the Canton Stand from the centre circle.

*Opposite top left:* Amusingly titled refreshment bar.

*Opposite top right:* The Canton Stand also housed disabled supporters at Ninian Park.

*Opposite bottom:* Canton Stand turnstiles from the inside.

117

THIS IS A
**FAMILY STAND**

PLEASE REFRAIN
FROM USING ·
COLOURFUL
LANGUAGE
AT ALL TIMES

PETER'S PIES PETER'S

*ve:* A sold out Canton Stand watches as Paul Parry takes a free kick against Arsenal in the FA Cup.

*osite far left:* Fans leaving the Canton Stand after the full time whistle.

*osite top right:* Snack bar on corner of Canton Stand and Grandstand.

*osite middle right:* A rule not always adhered to by parents and children alike.

*osite bottom right:* Canton Stand seating with executive boxes above.

## Chapter 9

# Farewell Ninian Park

I suppose we could have written the script in advance, but did our time at Ninian Park really have come to an end in such a gut-wrenching manner as it did on that Saturday in April 2009 when we lost 3-0 to Ipswich Town? In our previous home match, City had beaten Burnley 3-1 in a thrilling encounter that would have been a fitting end to the Ninian story. With just four league matches remaining, many of us believed we had already amassed enough points to secure a play-off spot and we still had an outside chance of clinching an automatic promotion place with the teams above us floundering.

I don't think anybody could have foreseen what was to happen in those last four games. A 6-0 hammering at Preston put paid to our automatic promotion chances, but a last-ditch equaliser at relegated Charlton gave us the point that almost guaranteed an extra game at Ninian Park after the regular season had ended. Even when we went down 3-0 to Ipswich in our final home league game, we still left the ground believing the play-offs were a formality.

Later that day, as the guests were starting to arrive at Glamorgan Cricket Club's SWALEC Stadium for the Cardiff City Supporters Club annual Player of the Year evening, news filtered through that Preston had grabbed an amazing last-minute winner at Birmingham, meaning we could still get caught on the final day of the season at Sheffield Wednesday. And, of course, the very worst happened at Hillsborough, cheating us out of one last finale at Ninian Park and a chance to say goodbye to the ground properly.

In hindsight, I'm glad that in many ways I treated the Ipswich game as our final match at Ninian. I arrived at the ground just after noon and, with camera in hand, I tried to capture everything about the day, asking random strangers for photos and chatting with fans about their feelings for the old place.

*Opposite:* Souvenir sellers prepare for one last Ninian Park encounter.

Some supporters were in fancy dress while others sported City kits from years gone by. Smiles sometimes turned to sadness as we reminisced about games past, but in the main it felt like a celebration of Ninian Park, our home of 99 years.

The game, of course, did nothing to maintain the mood. The Ipswich players were keen to impress their new manager, Roy Keane, and they romped to a comfortable 3-0 win, but not before Ross McCormack had missed an early penalty for City, squandering the chance to not only take the lead but also calm the nerves. The Bluebirds had completely outplayed the same team at Portman Road in December, but it seemed as if our players had run out of steam and effectively given up. After 42 games of being very hard to beat, it now appeared that City would roll over for anyone. Still, the players would pick themselves up and dust themselves down for the play-offs, wouldn't they?

As if to add insult to injury, the team trooped back onto the pitch after the end of the game for the 'Farewell to Ninian Park' celebrations wearing white t-shirts. Perhaps 'Farewell to Ninian Farce' would have been a more appropriate description of what followed. Machines were wheeled onto the pitch for what was supposed to be a state-of-the-art pyrotechnics display, but in truth there were more fireworks coming from the angry fans on the terraces.

To be fair, if the powers that be had organised an all-singing, all-dancing spectacular, it probably would have been criticised by the masses after the disappointment of the game we had just witnessed, but what we were served up with was an embarrassment.

Ali continued to play songs requested by the fans over the PA system, with Frank Sinatra's 'My Way' ringing around the stadium as the downbeat players trudged off the pitch and Ninian Park fell silent for the final time on a match day. But there was always that exciting play-off game to come, wasn't there?

Despite taking all those photos and treating the Ipswich game as our last, it didn't feel like it was the end and, to this day, I feel that I missed out on saying goodbye properly. I suppose I wanted to be the last person to leave Ninian after the final match, moved on by a steward or locked in after the gates were closed. In reality, I trudged out along with everyone else while 'My Way' faded into the distance. Thank you, Ninian Park. You managed to let me down one last time.

*Right:* Long before kick off, one final walk up Sloper Road to Ninian Park.

*Above:* Looking out from the main gates.

*Left:* John Perrett, programme seller and Ninian Park regular for many years.

*Above:* Ipswich are coming to spoil the party.

*Right:* All quiet at the main entrance.

*Top:* Turnstiles preparing to open for the last time.

TICKET
COLLECTION

BOOTH IN
CAR PARK
OPPOSITE

*Above:* Stewards await a sell out crowd.

*Right:* City fan Les Hayes, a regular at home and away games for many years.

*Above:* A desperate fan makes a plea for a spare ticket.

*Left:* Some City stewards were also part of the furniture at Ninian Park.

*Above:* John Maiwell was a regular around Ninian Park.

*Left:* Familiar faces chase autographs as Jay Bothroyd looks on.

*Opposite:* Ipswich fans pose for the camera, unaware that they would still be smiling after the match.

*Above:* Barry Doughty travelled down from the Lake District to pay homage one last time.

*Left:* Dark clouds gather on Sloper Road.

*Opposite:* For your City souvenirs, Billy 'Badges' has been the man to see for longer than he cares to remember.

*Above:* Clive Francis and Michael Lambert looking after the Supporters Club shop.

*Top:* Programme and Echo sellers united.

*Opposite:* City regular Ross Welch does the 'Ayatollah'.

137

*Above:* Richard and Beryl Fitzjohn are all smiles before kick off.

*Opposite:* Zoe Jones and son Jacob on Sloper Road.

*Above:* Vince Alm outside the Bob Bank turnstiles.

*Opposite:* Fans walking up Sloper Road.

141

*Above:* City fan Paul Randall in his Cardiff City kilt.

*Top left:* The South Wales Echo advertising their report.

*Middle left:* Terry Phillips preparing to report on his final match at Ninian Park.

*Bottom left:* The Morgan family have been supporting City for generations.

*Opposite:* Andrew Turton peddles his Thin Blue Line fanzine.

143

*Above:* My wife Irene with Grandstand regulars Sue Goodfriend & Liz Rogers.

*Right:* Nick Sheldon shifts a few copies of Watch The Bluebirds Fly.

*Opposite:* Even the police were all smiles.

*Above:* City's starting XI – Heaton, McNaughton, Kennedy, Johnson, Gyepes, Rae, Ledley, Parry, Burke, Bothroyd, McCormack.

*Left:* Heads down for the reporters in the Lower Grandstand.

*Above:* A marriage proposal at half time – luckily she said yes!

*Right:* Kick off.

*The Bob Bank waves farewell.*

*Fans stay for the after match celebrations despite the result.*

## Chapter 10

# The Fat Lady Sings

After the debacle of the Ipswich game and the subsequent failure to seal a play-off place on the final day of the season at Sheffield Wednesday, the club hastily tried to make amends for their failings, both on and off the pitch. To be fair, whatever they proposed, they could never really make up for the end-of-season capitulation we had all witnessed. Eventually, an open day dubbed 'the Party in the Park' was chosen instead of a final friendly or a Cardiff City legends game.

Despite many of us having reservations, the day was a success, with fans getting the opportunity to sit in their seats for one last time and even take a penalty in front of the Grange End. The rain did its best to spoil the day, but it didn't deter several thousand fans from paying their last respects to Ninian Park. The bars were selling off cheap beer and Cardiff players old and new were introduced to the crowd.

I spent a couple of hours wandering around all the stands, taking pictures of things I'd probably already photographed on numerous occasions. The day helped me feel as if I'd finally managed to say a sort of farewell to Ninian Park, but it wasn't to be my last visit to the old place. As the open day drew to a close, a crowd gathered on the Grange End, a congregation of City fans together for one final time at Ninian Park. Stewards, keen to lock the gates, tried to move them on, but the crowd just made their way onto the Bob Bank for another final song or two.

The following day, Ninian opened its doors for one last time to host a game with a team representing Cardiff City. It was a low-key legends game, already arranged by the charity Bobath Cymru, prior to the end of season turmoil. It was poorly advertised – I only found out about it thanks to a poster in a Canton pub – but it was a good day out and a few hundred diehard supporters turned up to watch some unfit and overweight heroes of the past take to the Ninian Park pitch again.

The City team included the likes of Jason Perry, Scott Young, Linden Jones, Keith Pontin and Cohen Griffith. We were treated to six goals, with five of them

coming from the legends and fittingly, it was a particular hero of mine, Carl Dale, who scored the final goal at Ninian Park by a player in a Cardiff City shirt. At the end of the game, I went onto the pitch and stood in the centre circle, taking in each stand one by one. This time, I really was told to get out by a steward who wanted to go home for his Sunday lunch. It still wasn't to be my last visit to Ninian Park though.

Over the course of the next couple of weeks, Ninian played host to a few regional football finals, as it had done many times over the years. A six-a-side tournament was also staged to give the fans one last opportunity to play on the pitch. Then an auction was held to sell off memorabilia and even some of the fixtures and fittings, so my next visit to Ninian Park was on a sunny Thursday morning to collect a gate from the front of the Bob Bank which now sits proudly in my garden.

I think a few of the auction winners were taken by surprise when they were told it was up to them to collect and remove the item they had won. Apparently it was in the small print, although I hadn't noticed it. So, armed with various tools and a mate in tow to provide some brute force, I walked across the pitch to my gate and then proceeded to hammer away the concrete of the Bob Bank wall that held the gate in place. At least I can claim to have played my part in demolishing Ninian Park. However, I pity the poor bloke who had to remove his clock from the Grange End roof!

By now, Ninian Park was beginning to look desperately sad. With signs and seats removed and parts of the terraces covered in rubble, the ground suddenly looked very much its 99 years. The pitch was almost brown, having been neglected by the groundsmen, who had a new pitch across the road to tend to.

The following weekend it was back to the Canton Suite for a book launch, with yet more signage missing around the ground and a brick structure appearing in the car park opposite, where the main gates from Ninian Park were to be moved to create a walkway to the new stadium.

Finally, I paid one last visit a week later to pick up my Grandstand seat, which now sits alongside my gate in my garden. Reading this, I guess you're probably thinking that I should get myself another hobby.

By that stage, the pitch had been completely removed and the bulldozers and diggers had moved in, ready to consign Ninian Park to memory. I was quite tearful while looking at the place for one final time, with large blocks of seats missing, crush barriers lying on the terraces and what used to be the pitch turned into mounds of earth. On 19th June 2009, the office staff began moving to their new home across the road and the final chapter of Ninian Park's 99-year history was complete.

I love watching football at the new stadium. All the things we moaned about at Ninian Park were soon forgotten as we got used to HD TV, overpriced hot food, cold beer and toilets that actually resemble toilets. We sit in comfortable seats which have plenty of legroom and excellent, unrestricted views of the action from every area.

But, despite all the good things the new stadium has brought us, the memories of the old ground still come flooding back from time to time. Radio Ninian in between the old Grange End and Grandstand, Golden Goal tickets, the disabled section at the corner of the Bob Bank and Canton Stand, the wooden benches, huge terraces, leaky roofs, terrible toilets, etc. The list goes on and on. The fat lady has long since sung her final song and the Ninian experience has gone forever, but for many of us it will never be forgotten. I'm sure even the most cynical Cardiff City supporter will find the time for an occasional moment of teary-eyed nostalgia now that Ninian Park has finally been flattened.

Farewell 'Our Ninian Park'.

*Opposite top:* May 2009 – Party In The Park, as fans gather for one more look around Ninian.

*Opposite bottom:* Lining up to take a penalty at the Grange End.

Above: Carl Dale sign authographs after scoring the final goal in a charity gar

Opposite top left: Even cardboard cutouts have to retire at some sta

Opposite top right: The more cynical fans amongst us thought it should read 'End Of An Err

Opposite bottom: Standing on the Grange End one last ti

*Above:* A member of the groundstaff gets to work with an angle grinder.

*Top:* James Fox performs at the End Of An Era dinner at the Vale Of Glamorgan Hotel.

*Right:* Irene and myself on the Ninian Pitch.

*Above:* June 2009 – The diggers arrive as the pitch is removed.

*Top:* Ninian Park – reflecting on better days?

*Left:* The Bob Bank looking worse for wear.

163

Above: The Lower Grandstand becomes a terrace once m...

Opposite top left: The view from the tu...

Opposite top right: Seats being removed from the Canton S...
– many of which were donated to Chasetow...

Opposite bottom: In days gone by they'd have played football or...

*Above:* The Grange End is torn

*Left:* The Grandstand witnesses a mud

*Top:* October 2009 – The new home for the Ninian Park

*Opposite:* As the cladding on the Grandstand was rem
the original lettering was revealed on the brickwork be

*Above:* A floodlight, minus its lamps.

*Top:* The souvenir shop becomes the new site office for Redrow.

*Right:* The Grandstand, prior to demolition.

*Opposite:* The Bob Bank does it best to rise above the rubble.

*Above:* Just a handful of seats remain.

*Top:* Rubble mounts up in front of the Grandstand.

*Left:* The end is in sight for Ninian Park.

171

*Above:* Removing the roof supports.

*Right:* October 2009 – The Grandstand roof falls to the ground.

Timber!

Above: Housing plots marked out on the pitch.

Top: November 2009 – Sloper Road will never look the same again.

Right: May 2010 – New housing where a football ground once stood.

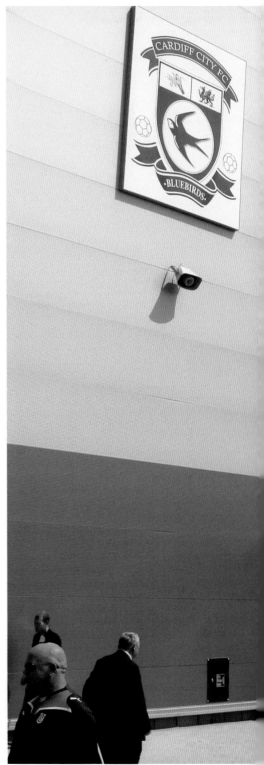

*Above:* Inside our new home – here's to the next 99 years.

*Right:* August 2009 – The Cardiff City Stadium, all shiny & new.

# My Ninian Park

By Gwilym Rees

" Stood in the terraced enclosure on a fruit box behind the manager's dug out and just about able to see over the wall, I had a worm's-eye view of the surroundings "

My first ever visit to Ninian Park was on Boxing Day 1967 as an impressionable eight year old. We beat Aston Villa 3-0 and I can remember City striker Bobby Brown was seriously injured in front of the Grange End.

Stood in the terraced enclosure on a fruit box behind the manager's dug out and just about able to see over the wall, I had a worm's-eye view of the surroundings. I remember being mesmerized by the crowd, watching hundreds of fans running and charging back and forth between the Grange End and the Bob Bank. The ones in claret and blue seemed to be the fastest from what I could see.

Today, when I listen to the tales of the massive Cardiff games of yesteryear, I can't contribute to those conversations because I wasn't allowed to go if massive crowds were expected. However, I can say 'I was there' for Oswestry, Stourbridge and Worcester in the Welsh Cup.

I think the 1975/76 season was probably my favourite as a Bluebird and it was also the year when the team wore my favourite kit – the one with a yellow and white stripe down one side of the blue shirt. The club had made some impressive signings such as Mike England, the great Tottenham and Wales centre half, striker Tony Evans, Aussie international Adrian Alston and midfielder Doug Livermore. There were some epic games that season. Hereford at home springs to mind with at least 35,000 in attendance and this time 'I was there' to see us beat the side that were top of the league.

I lived away from Cardiff for most of the 80's and 90's and my trips to Ninian Park were reduced to just a handful per season. With the team and the stadium deteriorating it was a sad sight and I found Ninian Park without the old Grange End soulless.

My own circumstances changed and with an eight year-old son keen on football, we became season ticket holders in 1998. Promotion to the Second Division was quickly followed by relegation back to the dungeon, but I was pleased my son was hooked, probably by the passion of the fans – the same passion that had hooked me many years before.

Attendances were on the up during the last couple of seasons at Ninian Park and the fans created a special atmosphere. On occasions, all four sides of the ground were in full voice and the stadium was regularly close to capacity. As we know, it all ended in tears. I didn't stay on for the end-of-season celebration after the disastrous defeat by Ipswich. I couldn't see the point. After all, we would all be going back for a play-off game a couple of weeks later, wouldn't we?

# My Ninian Park

By Dave Sugarman

For many Cardiff fans, it seemed that leaving Ninian Park was a real wrench, but I didn't share such feelings. The way some have waxed lyrical about Ninian, you'd be forgiven for thinking the Bluebirds had a glorious recent history, but the truth is that great occasions at the ground were few and far between.

My father took me to my first-ever Cardiff game in March 1975 on the day before my eighth birthday. City's opponents, Sheffield Wednesday, were rock bottom of the Second Division, while the Bluebirds were just one place above them. Predictably, the match ended goalless. The crowd of 6,621 jeered and chanted 'what a load of rubbish' at regular intervals. Both teams were relegated a month later. Nevertheless, I was still bitten by the Bluebirds bug.

I pleaded with dad to buy me a season ticket for the 1975/76 campaign. We sat in the back row of the Grandstand and I have great memories from my first full season. The likes of Willie Anderson, Adrian Alston and Tony Evans played some brilliant football as they fired the Bluebirds to promotion. The team also included a couple of my all-time favourite Cardiff players in the shape of John Buchanan and Phil Dwyer.

By the time Rick Wright arrived at the club in 1991, the ground was in a pathetic state. He made some significant improvements and he also briefly improved the team. The 1992/93 Third Division championship campaign still rates as my favourite in all my years following Cardiff. The squad Eddie May put together included some real heroes like Carl Dale, Phil Stant, Jason Perry, Nathan Blake, Paul Ramsey, Cohen Griffith and Robbie James.

Something that always amuses me in relation to Ninian Park is the persistent claims that the ground had an intimidating atmosphere. Of course, when the ground was full for big cup games against the likes of Manchester City and Leeds United, the atmosphere certainly was intimidating, but such occasions were the exceptions to the rule.

I was flicking through the record books a while back and was surprised to discover that I'd been amongst Ninian crowds that were smaller than 1,000 on no less than fifteen separate occasions. Admittedly, most of those games were minor Welsh Cup or FAW Premier Cup ties, but some are still fresh in my memory, as are home defeats by the likes of Aldershot, Barnet, Bath, Chester, Merthyr and Weymouth.

The Bluebirds have been an established Championship side since 2003, and at long last the club has a ground to match its Football League status. Ninian Park was a dilapidated dinosaur from a bygone age and I'm glad it is finally extinct.

> " I pleaded with dad to buy me a season ticket for the 1975/76 campaign. We sat in the back row of the Grandstand and I have great memories from my first full season "

## My Ninian Park

By Paul Stephens

Ninian Park for me means memories going back over forty years to my schooldays. Starting off in the early 70's, standing on the Grange End with mates from the old Cardiff High School, smoking Consulate, Embassy or whatever we could get our hands on and then the football special back to Llanishen from Ninian Park Halt. These were the Toshack and Clark years and a vivid memory still exists of Barrie Jones coming down the wing in front of the Bob Bank.

The ground back then had a magic era about it, especially during night games and I well remember a match against Swindon over the Christmas period in the early 70's when the pitch was covered with snow and Don Murray was a gladiator in central midfield. I still remember Freda Payne's 'Band of Gold' being played on Radio Ninian and echoing around the terraces.

My other link to Ninian Park in the 70's was earning money. My late father was a freelance press photographer in Cardiff and covered the City from the 50's through until his retirement in 1993.

During the period from 1972-1976 while a student at Bristol University, I used to come home when I could for City games and work for my Dad taking action pictures from behind the line. It was good fun entering the ground through the main entrance, having a pre-match drink in the lounge with the other pressmen, before taking up our position about 20 yards from the posts. We usually only got to see 20-30 minutes of the first half and hoped for some good action pictures in this time. The films would then be rushed back to his darkroom in Charles Street, processed and then transmitted over telephone line for subsequent publication in the Sunday Nationals. It was quite a buzz to see one of your pictures on the back of the Sunday Express!

As well as City games, we also attended the home internationals and I can remember seeing Gordon Banks, Bobby Moore, Colin Bell and Malcolm Macdonald when England really was a great side. My father also had a very close relationship with the management setup and members of the team, and he knew legendary manager Jimmy Scoular and Tosh and his family.

My last game at Ninian was during the mid 70's and I wasn't to return until some 25 years later with my youngsters when Cardiff had a cup replay against Reading. We sat in the family enclosure which in those days was in front of the Grandstand. The kids loved it and that was to be the start of my return to Ninian Park, with all three of them in tow as they became avid City fans themselves despite us living just south of Reading.

" During the period from 1972-1976 while a student at Bristol University, I used to come home when I could for City games and work for my Dad taking action pictures from behind the line "

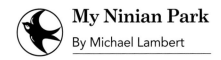

# My Ninian Park

By Michael Lambert

I was just twelve years old when I went to the City v Arsenal FA Cup third round tie at Ninian, and was completely stunned by the 55,136 crowd, the noise, the colours and smells of a big match day. I fell in love with the Bluebirds there and then.

The match was goalless but the memories of Brian Clark storming the Arsenal defence, helped by a stringy youngster named John Toshack, have lived with me ever since. I sat on the Bob Bank wall, clinging on for dear life as the famous names of Arsenal struggled against the Second Division challengers. A few years ago against Wigan I went on the Bob Bank terrace with my young stepson, standing a few yards back as he sat on the very same section of wall.

Of course, only my first few years as a City fan were spent following a team that looked destined to reach the First Division. For two more seasons we watched as City developed into real challengers and John Toshack became an international striker. Then disaster – after a hat-trick against Hull in October 1970 he left for Liverpool, and it broke my heart when Shankly stole him for a pittance. Meanwhile City's challenge was cruelly ended by Watford at Ninian on a sunny April afternoon. Many cite the 5-1 defeat at Sheffield United as killing our challenge off but it was that 1-0 defeat that really did the damage. The joy of beating Real Madrid and all that has been written about that night disappeared in a puff of smoke when the First Division was lost that day.

There are plenty of good things to remember – 1976 when we had 35,000 for a Third Division match against Hereford; the Tottenham, Wrexham and Everton FA Cup games in 1977; the heady days of ninth place in the Second Division in 1978/79 and the promotion seasons of 1982/83, 1987/88 and 1992/93 are all still as fresh in my mind as if they were last year.

But the bad memories, such as 4-0 defeats by Fulham in the league and Merthyr in the Welsh Cup, a 5-0 drubbing by Maidstone, a 7-2 hammering by Cambridge and FA Cup defeats by Weymouth and Bath City, are too many and too gloomy to relate here. The record low attendance of 1,334 against Hartlepool definitely belongs here.

What about the characters? Well, for me, there is only one. Harry Parsons personified Cardiff City throughout four decades, starting in the Sixties when he first helped out at the club. Harry was a man who, even on the darkest of days at Ninian Park, would always have a smile and a joke for anyone who drew near. City through and through, I miss him still.

> " The match was goalless but the memories of Brian Clark storming the Arsenal defence, helped by a stringy youngster named John Toshack, have lived with me ever since "

" My final favourite
memories will be
of Ross McCormack
smashing home the
injury time penalty
against Watford,
where the roar must
have been heard
miles away "

## My Ninian Park
By Matthew Gabb

The first games I went to at Ninian Park were in the 1993/94 season. Eddie May was the manager, and the City side contained fans favourites like Phil Stant, Carl Dale, Nathan Blake and Jason Perry. The league season failed to deliver, but City had a great FA Cup run. After disposing of Enfield and Brentford in the first two rounds, we were drawn against Middlesbrough at home in the third round.

What seemed like an enormous crowd of 13,750 packed into a rainy Ninian Park. We went behind and came back twice, first through Stant, and second late on through a Garry Thompson toe poke. The final score was 2-2. I stood in an overcrowded Canton Stand in the aisle and looked on in awe at fans slipping and sliding onto the muddy pitch in celebration of the equaliser.

We went on to win the replay at Ayresome Park and faced Manchester City in round four. Plenty has been written about that particular game, but I remember the ticket rush as much as anything. A friend from school got mine for me – a £5 Bob Bank terrace juvenile ticket. We won the game in splendid circumstances, the winning goal from Nathan Blake curled jubilantly past City keeper Tony Coton, followed by Mark Grew saving a penalty in front of the Grange End.

The 1995/96 and 1997/98 seasons saw us notch up two all-time low league positions. Plenty of my memories of Ninian Park are of watching City in front of less than 3,000 people, scrambling around for points against teams like Halifax and Scarborough.

The last few years at Ninian Park were some of the most memorable. The obvious highlights being a win against top of the Premiership Leeds in the FA Cup and the play-off semi-final victory against Bristol City. However, these were interspersed with the shocking 2-0 home defeat to Stoke in the play-offs. That's one that I think still registers as the biggest disappointment I've felt watching City. I can still hear the melancholy tones of Abba's 'The Winner Takes It All' as we shuffled out of the ground.

My final favourite memories will be of Ross McCormack smashing home the injury time penalty against Watford, where the roar must have been heard miles away. But finally it will be the last five minutes of the Burnley game on Easter Monday 2009, where we scored twice late on to win 3-1. It all went wrong after that, but for one day only it seemed like nothing could stand in our way.

And I've still got a little bit of Ninian Park, row F of the Directors box seats will be sitting in pride of place in my garden for years to come.

# My Ninian Park

By Clive Francis

It's over forty years since I first went to Ninian Park. My parents were interested in the wrong shaped ball and had no real love of football. Part of the problem was that crowd disorder and violence had started to creep into the game in the early 70's and then Manchester United came to town in 1974 and all hell broke loose. Eventually they threw the towel in and accepted that Cardiff City would be part of their lives whether they liked it or not.

It was actually left to my friend's father to take me to my first game at the tender age of ten and to him I will always be eternally grateful. I remember very little about the game itself, only the experience of being there and, in particular, the atmosphere. My mate was a couple of years older than me and I remember asking him what the Grange End fans were chanting to the away supporters. He leaned over and whispered in my ear 'they're singing you're gonna get your f*****g heads kicked in'!

As a young lad I'd catch the bus on the A48 and alight at the Central Bus Station rather than get off in Canton. I loved the walk out to the ground, getting your chips en-route, sellers trying to flog Golden Goal tickets on Sloper Road, pie and Bovril at half time. It was all part of the day.

> " I loved the walk out to the ground, getting your chips en-route, sellers trying to flog Golden Goal tickets on Sloper Road, pie and Bovril at half time. It was all part of the day "

Over the years I've had the privilege to watch some fine players perform in a City shirt, the likes of Murray, Gibson, Buchanan, Dwyer, Dale, Ratcliffe, Blake, Stant and Earnshaw to name a few. Like many, I've witnessed both fantastic and diabolical performances from City sides. Some of the highlights for me personally have been the FA Cup ties against Manchester City in 1993, Leeds in 2002, the last minute draw against Swansea in 1980, the 4-1 hiding West Ham took a few years back and the incredible 5-4 win against Plymouth in the Littlewoods Cup in 1986.

On the down side, the mid 80's in particular were a difficult time. Thankfully, unlike many of my friends, I kept going despite the relegations, dismal performances and the deterioration of the ground. If I am honest, if I had stopped going then I don't know if I would have gone back and that's why I stuck it out. I always held on to the thought that things would get better.

As much as I loved Ninian Park, after 99 years the ground was simply past its sell-by date. It will though always hold a special place in my heart. I will miss her, never forget her and will always remember her fondly.

Thanks for all the memories.

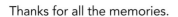

## My Ninian Park

By Rob Davies

They say your first visit to Ninian Park is memorable but in many respects it was my second one, Wales v England in 1961. Although I don't remember much, I do recall being passed to the back of the Bob Bank to get a view from the wall! Apparently my first trip was for a City draw against Blackburn Rovers but that one has long gone from the memory banks.

During the early to mid 60's, I probably saw more Wales games there than Cardiff City. I remember Wales 3 Scotland 2 with Ken Leek (who? I hear you say) scoring two late goals; England winning after the World Cup in late '66; and Luigi Riva getting the only goal in a defeat to Italy.

At the start of the 1968/69 season, I was allowed to go on my own and the alliance was forged forever. Little did I know that those early Scoular years would be the best for a while and Ninian Park would became my second home for the next forty years. The Saturday routine was bus from Cwmbran to Newport; train to Cardiff; walk along Tudor Street (chips en route) and get to the ground in time to see the players arrive; on the Grange End by 1.45 – same barrier and same friends that I only met once every two weeks.

During the 70's when I was at university and worked in London I managed only a handful of games at Ninian Park, notably the memorable games against Real Madrid, Crystal Palace and Hereford. I started to go on a more regular basis again in the late 80's when my eldest Gavin started to show an interest. His early hero was Jimmy Gilligan and the supply of sweets never lasted long enough whilst running around a sparsely populated Bob Bank.

The successful 92/93 season was the start of his brother Chris joining us and until university and parenthood beckoned, my daughter Amy made it a family foursome. The 90's were a time when Ninian Park meant a family day out and come win, lose or draw, we always looked forward with anticipation to the next visit. The moving family section resulted in us sampling all areas of Ninian Park and they enjoyed collecting autographs by the tunnel, before the inevitable teenage years spent on the Grange End.

The last 8 years at Ninian Park saw crowds return to the 1960's/70's levels and with it, the intimidating atmosphere, especially for floodlit games, that brought us added points and cup success. The bumper crowds of the final years were a fitting send off for our home and will live long in the memory of the Davies family and City fans everywhere.

Thank you Ninian Park – gone, but never forgotten.

# ACKNOWLEDGEMENTS

Thanks to my wife Irene for her assistance in proof-reading and to Dave Sugarman for his attention to detail in making sure all the facts and figures contained within this publication are (hopefully!) accurate and for providing me with his excellent 'Brief History of Ninian Park' piece.

Thank you to all of the contributors for putting down their own memories of Ninian Park and to Paul Stephens, Jon Candy and Brian Mertens for kindly allowing me to use their photos which helped to fill a few gaps in my own collection.

Finally, I'd like to express my gratitude to Rob, Mark and Ant at Wyndcliff, who provided invaluable help in turning my original draft into reality and to the committee of Cardiff City Supporters Club for their support in funding this project. Thanks guys.

*Profits from the sale of this book will be donated to the Fred Keenor Statue Appeal*